BEDMaR & SHi:

The Bali Villas

BEDMaR & SHi: The Bali Villas

Edited by Oscar Riera Ojeda
Text by Darlene Smyth
Photography by Albert Lim

OSCAR RIERA OJEDA
PUBLISHERS

Contents

Acknowledgements
10

Introduction
12

01. The Project
18

02. Drawings
168

03. Site and Construction
182

04. Project Data
192

05. Biography
194

Acknowledgements

by Ernesto Bedmar

When I was first commissioned to build this villa in Bali, a strong feeling of insecurity overcame me; I have always admired Balinese architecture for its simplicity, spontaneity and the Balinese culture which treasures religion, nature and art above anything else. Surrounded by today's globalized world and highly intellectual forms and interpretations of design, it was difficult to get back to basics and isolate myself from the trends and competition of colleagues creating projects on my beloved island of Bali. Once again, I allowed myself to be led by the images and emotions that Bali and the site aroused within me; embracing the essence of the land and aiming at nothing more ambitious than the creation of a simple, almost traditional composition of pavilions surrounded by a compound wall and a gate. 'BIG GATE' is an essential element of a true 'Oriental Garden.' It is the sea, walls and water features which create

My appreciation goes to Rahul Mookerjee, my client, who trusted and deposited confidence in me to build a simple environment for his holiday home. To Shinta Siregar and Trevor Hiller who knew the local context far better than me; their input was invaluable. To all the consultants whose contributions were crucial in various aspects of the project, and to the contractor and artisans who did remarkable work in record time. To all the people in my office who worked on the project, to Oscar Riera Ojeda for his perseverance in coping with my bad character and trusting me one more time. To Darlene Smyth and Albert Lim for once again contributing to the book with their writing and photography respectively. Finally, to all the gods and spirits of Bali who after this project blessed me with 3 new commissions on the island.

The Bali Villas

Introduction by Darlene Smyth

The seemingly endless rhythm of open fronted roadside stalls selling locally made crafts and products slowly begins to decrease in frequency toward the outskirts of the famous shopping region of Seminyak. At first, glimpses of more distant mountains and fields can be seen through the openings between these simple buildings lined against the small country road. The almost surreal, intense green of the tropical sun-washed landscape of palm trees and rice fields overwhelms the senses. This is the Bali so often captured in paintings and batik prints, the beautifully terraced rice paddies with ripe crops gently blowing in the warm wind and the ominous black earth and stone reminding the villagers of the silent power of the volcanoes on the horizon. The haunting beauty of this place and its culturally rich architecture has deeply influenced much of the career of Ernesto Bedmar, who runs his design practice in the busy tropical city state of Singapore, just a few hours' flight away. Yet the commission of the Jiva Puri villa in Bali to Bedmar & Shi was the Argentinian-born designer's first long awaited opportunity to execute his designs on the island itself. The slow journey to the villa, with its gradual paring down of all forms of urbanization is an integral part of the physical and mental preparation required to open the senses to the villa and to its intricate connection to the built history and dramatic landscape of the southwestern Balinese coastline.

After turning off the main road into one of the many narrow neighborhood streets, the atmosphere changes once again. Young children play freely along the quiet roadside near a series of dark volcanic stone temples with traditional Balinese figures carved into every surface. With minimal warning, a large gateway appears to the left of the road, marking the understated entrance to the villa. From here, Bedmar brings the visitor on a carefully choreographed journey through the site, on which the architecture, open spaces, vistas and gateways all act in unison to allow for the gradual uncovering of the subtleties, the mysteries and the dramatic beauty of the site and its surroundings. The journey through the grounds is also planned with an understanding of the traditional Balinese architecture of a residential compound and the concepts and belief systems that regulate the arrangement of spaces and pavilions within it. Much of Balinese everyday life is linked to a common belief system of rituals and mythology that remains very strong in society to this day. Concepts that govern the traditional arrangement of the housing compound relate to a belief in the importance of a cosmological ordering of elements, as well as the path of the sun and the axis of the mountains and the sea. In Balinese belief, the cosmological order is derived from the map of Bali, which is seen as a microcosm of the whole of the cosmos. Since the holy Mount Agung is in the Northeast of the island, this cardinal direction is seen as being more sacred and is where the temple of each compound would be placed. The center of the island is seen as a transitional zone, so the middle of the housing compound is traditionally left open as a field or courtyard. Toward the South and Southwest is the sea which is associated with the sunset, with death, and with the profane. Bedmar & Shi have understood and reinterpreted these associations in the planning of the Jiva Puri.

From the street, the villa is almost completely hidden from the spectator by a tall boundary wall. The fence around a property is referred to in Bali as "angkul-angkul" and is thought to protect the inhabitants as well as help control the views into the property. The visitor enters the grounds through a tall, narrow gateway. At The Jiva Puri, this gateway has been simplified by omitting the traditional carved stone detailing, yet the traditional proportions of the entrance gateway have been retained. Through this narrow opening, Bedmar is able to control how much to reveal and how much to conceal. The experience of the villa and the gardens is delayed by the gateway and slowed to the pace of the movement of the body through the space as opposed to what can be captured in the quick glance of an eye. This controlled revelation and uncovering of the site is orchestrated by Bedmar in a manner that focuses the attention on the long, carefully composed vistas and spatial arrangements, making it possible to appreciate the subtleties of the architecture and landscape at each turn.

The view from the entrance gateway comes as a bit of a surprise. After travelling along a narrow roadway where the eye is focusing on objects and scenes within a few meters distance from the vehicle, Bedmar & Shi then reward the visitor with a very long, stretched out, almost one point perspective across a simple open field to the next gateway in the distance. This perspective is accentuated by a long white stone path down its center, leading to a bright opening in the wall of the villa beyond. To the left of the path is a simply-planted open field, reminiscent of the open, transitional center of traditional Balinese housing compounds. To the right is a series of black ponds with branching paths leading to four separate sleeping pavilions for invited guests. Fully bloomed Frangipani trees cast beautiful shadows on the simple white stone of the paths. The architectural elements of the path; the plain white walls, the pure shapes of the pavilions, are all pared down to their simplest form. This allows the decoration of the vistas to be the shadows and textures of the trees, and the rippled reflections the water casts across the surfaces of the walls.

Due to the strong contrast between the light stone of the path and the darker lawn and black ponds, the path appears almost to float, evoking a feeling of lightness and peace within the visitor. As the paths traverse the ponds, this illusion of floatation is further enhanced by the detail of the thin edge of stone along the sides of the path that projects beyond the recessed supports. These recessed edges create dark shadow lines under the stone slabs, making them appear as though they are hovering over the water. This simple but elegant detail of a groove between materials is continued throughout The Jiva Puri where Bedmar expresses but simplifies the connections between materials with grooves, recesses and shadow lines, gently marking the transitions between spaces and building elements. The side walls of the four sleeping villas that border the central field are treated in a similar way to the external walls of the compound. These walls not only provide privacy, but become the canvas for the shadows and texture of Frangipani trees that emerge from the ponds in small planters. A natural bio-filtration system in these ponds makes them appear as if they

naturally erupted there, and also gives the water an impossibly black and reflective quality. The darkness and reflectivity of the ponds furthers the impression that the buildings and pathways float above them. Bedmar & Shi deliberately construct vistas and visual perspectives to bring the visitors into the bedroom villas which are here controlled by the bounding walls of the villa along the white paths to frame the views as one passes through the sets of walls. Several of these framed views use linear "artworks" along the end walls of the view, to create attractive compositions as well as to stretch the eye around the edge of the framed view toward the next direction of travel. Upon closer examination, these linear artworks are in fact carefully chosen pieces taken from traditional Balinese buildings, such as carved roof eave details, and weathered timber columns.

In keeping with the simplification of architectural elements and forms in the project, the traditional heavy-looking thatched Balinese roof is here reinterpreted using light grey wooden shingles and exposed Balau timber rafters on the undersides of the roof with bamboo mat ceilings between them. The edge of the roof eave is made much slimmer than the traditional Bali villa by projecting the battens off the ends of the rafters and edging them with a thin timber fascia. The ends of the rafters are cut parallel to the ground so that the whole eave appears to come almost to a sharp point that conceals its actual thickness. Bedmar plays with the impression of the heaviness of the massive roof by abstracting its edge to make it appear almost paper-thin.

This same illusion also occurs inside the sleeping pavilions where the walls are lifted so that they almost meet the roof but then stop short in order to recess and conceal the connection. Again, the massive roof appears to float above the walls. This impression is also accentuated by the artificial lighting in the four corners of the rooms which up-light the underside of the ceiling, giving it a magical lightness. The intricacy of the detailing and local craftsmanship of these ceilings starkly contrasts with the simplicity of the plain white internal walls of the pavilions, once again turning the craftsmanship into a form of artwork set against a blank canvas.

As one moves from the larger open space of the central field into the realm of the sleeping pavilions, there is a deliberate scaling down of nature from the open public common center to a semi-public rock garden shared in between the four pavilions, and then to a private garden outside the bedroom of each villa. At each stage of the decreasing scale of the gardens, the designer has also brought the natural elements closer and closer to the visitor so that the small plantings and pond outside the bedrooms feel very personal, almost as if they were a childhood memory of a favorite corner of the garden. The last stage of the progressive scaling down of the gardens is in the semi-outdoor bathrooms behind the bedrooms where nature literally touches the visitor. Here, the plants are within close reach and the raindrops are felt as part of the cleansing ritual. Upon exiting the bedroom villas, the visitor is faced with a simple, long wall and covered walkway at the opposite side of the central field.

This wall conceals the service and cooking areas behind as well as the more private owner's pavilion which is tucked away at the Southeastern corner of the site. This larger structure enjoys the privacy of being set apart from the other guest bedroom pavilions and is also projected out toward the ocean to provide a view of the spectacular sunsets across the open sea.

The culmination of the series of vistas from the main entrance gates across the central field opens into the side of the living and dining pavilions. Unlike the sleeping villas, these longer pavilions are completely open-sided and use tall and richly weathered iron-wood or ulin columns recycled from old jetties, electricity poles and rail sidings built during the period of Dutch colonization in Indonesia. The high, slim proportions of these supports, along with the massive span of the cleverly designed timber roof trusses, gives the living space a sense of grandeur through proportion and scale without resorting to overly elaborate detailing. Should the weather not be favorable for the open living and dining pavilions, the inhabitant can take refuge in a glass-sided library and spa to the West of the main living spaces. This pavilion is again surrounded by water but here has more the feeling of a lagoon since the edges of the water body are more naturally profiled to the undulating landscape. All the furniture pieces and lighting in the villa were designed by Bedmar & Shi. These furniture elements fully take advantage of and accentuate the refined but relaxed atmosphere of the villa and also echo the stretched linearity of the framed views into the spaces.

An eight-seat-long sofa is aligned with the back of the living room and faces the beautiful front garden. A seven-meter-long distressed wood dining table is spanned by nine giant suspended lanterns made of inverted timber strip fishing traps. All the materials and craftsmanship used in these pieces were locally sourced and include thematic elements such as carved timber reclining chairs and an anvil-like stool and side table carved from the locally abundant black stone.

From the entrance of the living pavilion, the visitor is overwhelmed with a spectacular view of the wide-open ocean and horizon. This part of the ocean to the Southwest of Bali is known as being particularly active with large crashing waves along the black sand beaches and is the perfect dramatic visual climax to the journey through the compound. A historic Hindu temple made from carved black volcanic stone is built out into the dark ocean and creates a mystical backdrop for the sunsets from The Jiva Puri Villa. As the living room is much higher than sea-level, Bedmar stretched out a long tension edge swimming pool in the foreground, reaching toward the sea so that it appears to seamlessly merge with the water of the ocean. For the lawn next to this pool, the perimeter planting is carefully raised to conceal the transition to the ocean. The lawn itself steps downward in wide shallow platforms, reminiscent of the rice paddies outside. This gradual terracing of the lawn creates a form of amphitheater so that the inhabitants of The Jiva Puri can rest and enjoy the magnificent ocean view.

/01 The Project

Main pedestrian entry gate.

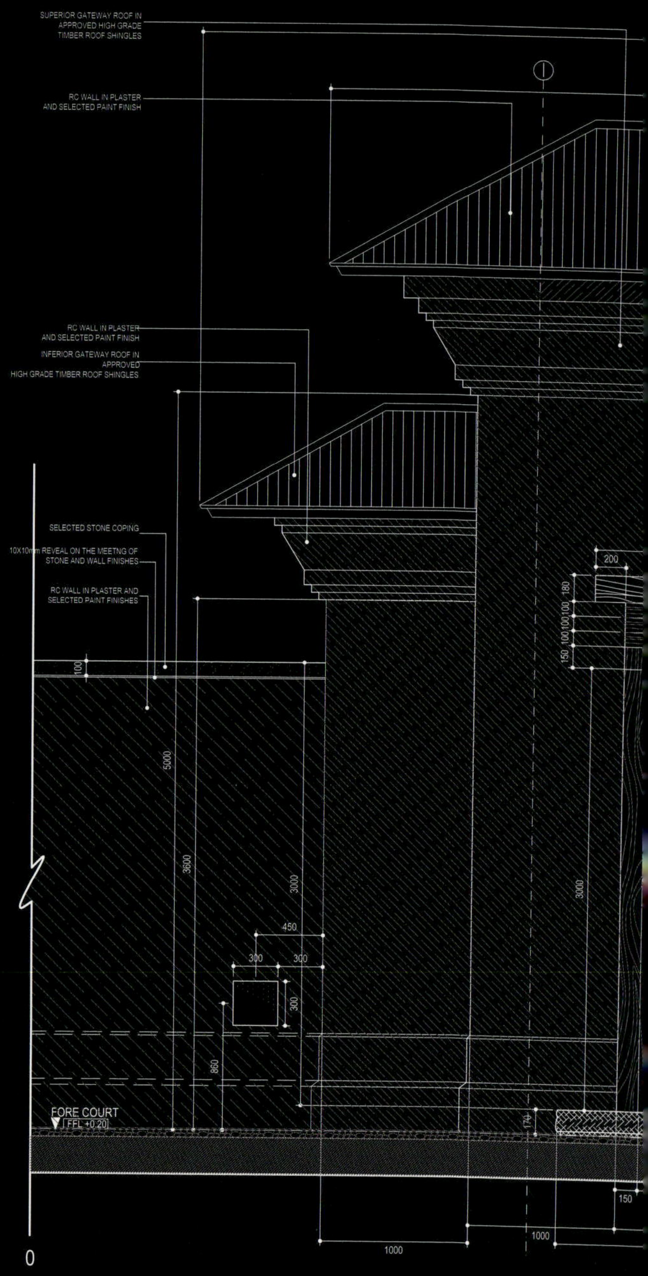

View of the Court with the main pavilion at the end and the sea beyond.

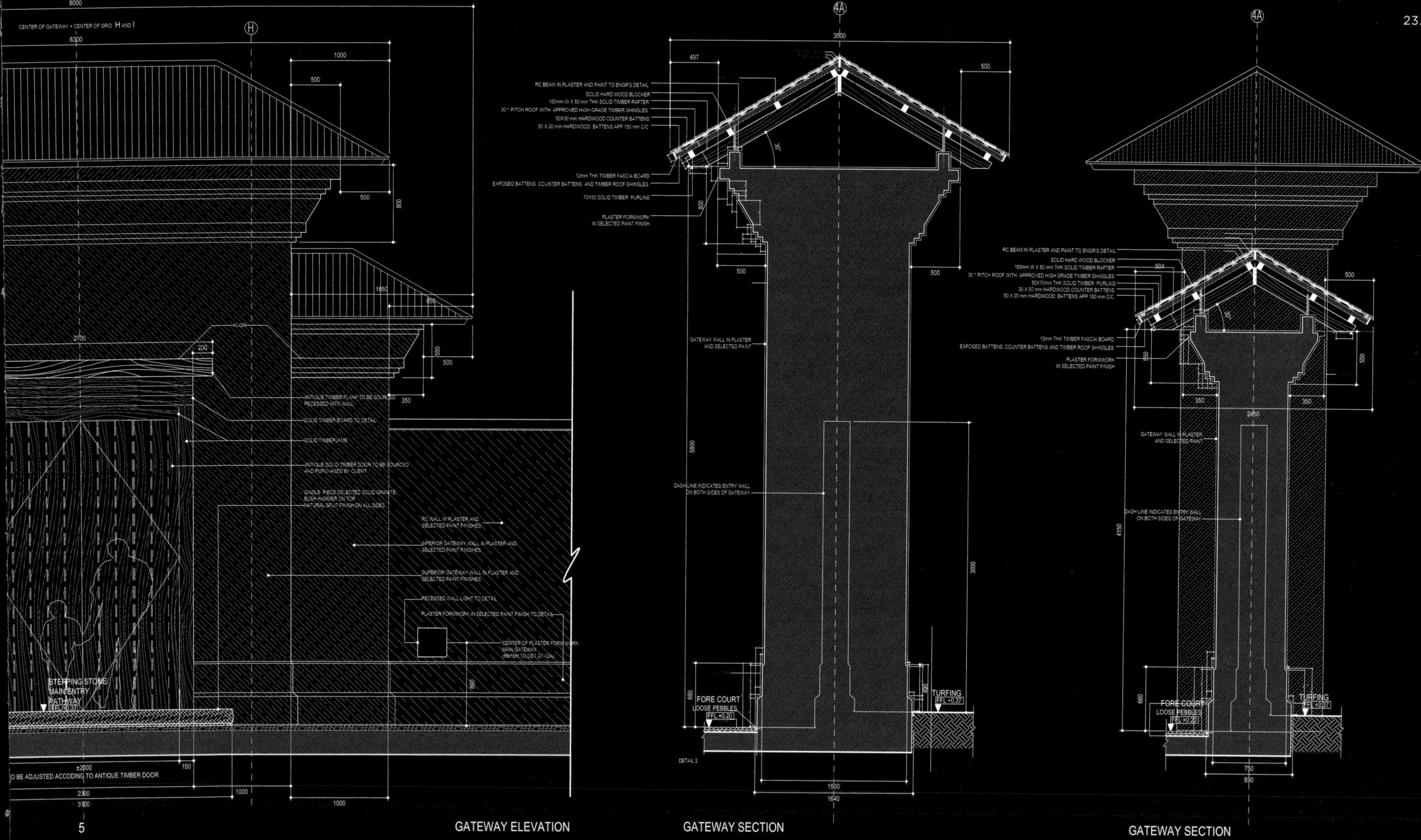

Secondary gateway details.

View of pond and walls enclosing the private gardens of the Guest Pavilions.

View of covered circulation & decorative local art & craft object.

View of covered circulation & decorative local art & craft object.

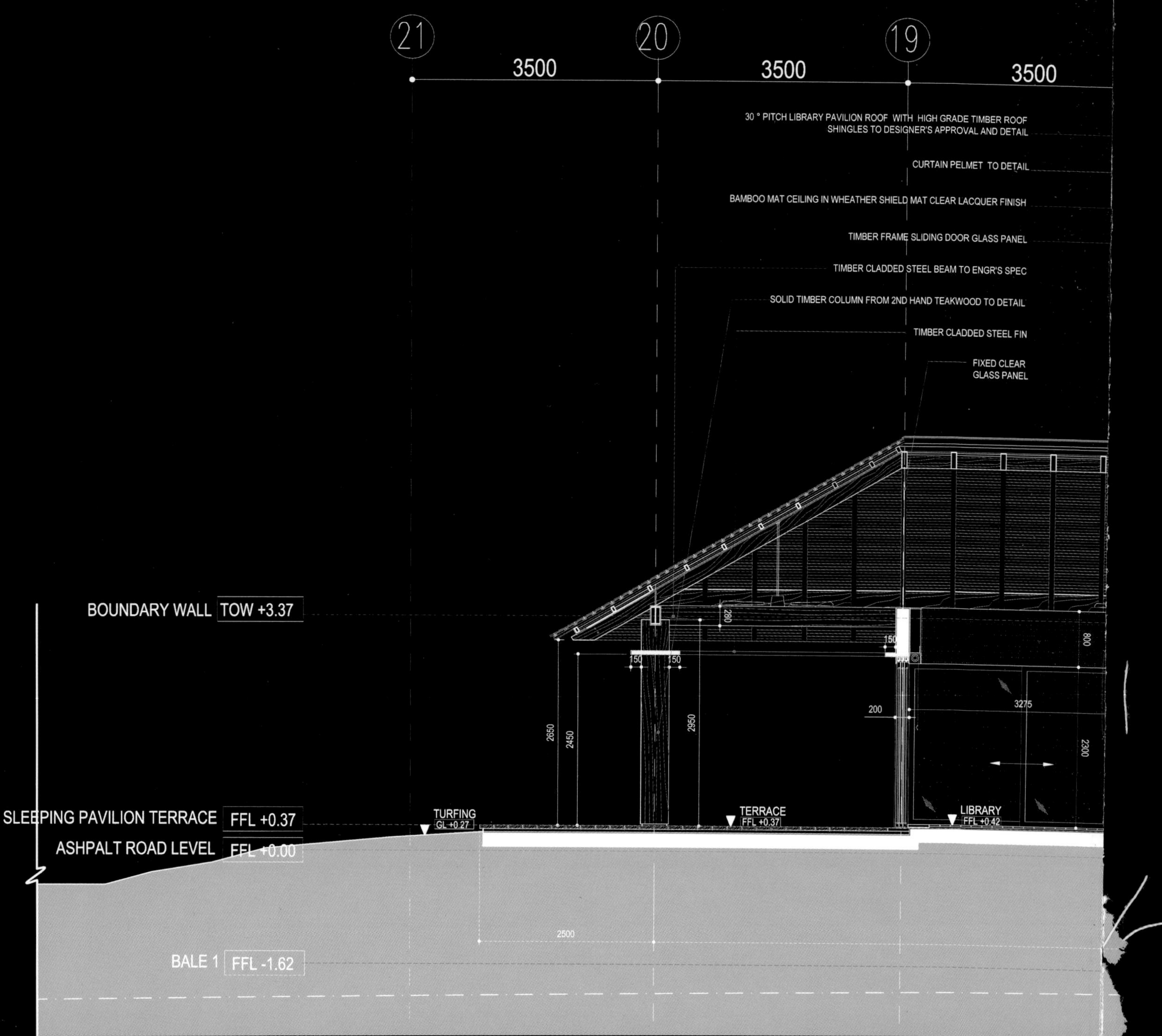
21
20
19
3500
3500
3500
30 ° PITCH LIBRARY PAVILION ROOF WITH HIGH GRADE TIMBER ROOF SHINGLES TO DESIGNER'S APPROVAL AND DETAIL
CURTAIN PELMET TO DETAIL
BAMBOO MAT CEILING IN WHEATHER SHIELD MAT CLEAR LACQUER FINISH
TIMBER FRAME SLIDING DOOR GLASS PANEL
TIMBER CLADDED STEEL BEAM TO ENGR'S SPEC
SOLID TIMBER COLUMN FROM 2ND HAND TEAKWOOD TO DETAIL
TIMBER CLADDED STEEL FIN
FIXED CLEAR GLASS PANEL
BOUNDARY WALL TOW +3.37
280
150
150
150
800
200
3275
2650
2450
2950
2300
SLEEPING PAVILION TERRACE FFL +0.37
ASHPALT ROAD LEVEL FFL +0.00
TURFING GL +0.27
TERRACE FFL +0.37
LIBRARY FFL +0.42
2500
BALE 1 FFL -1.62

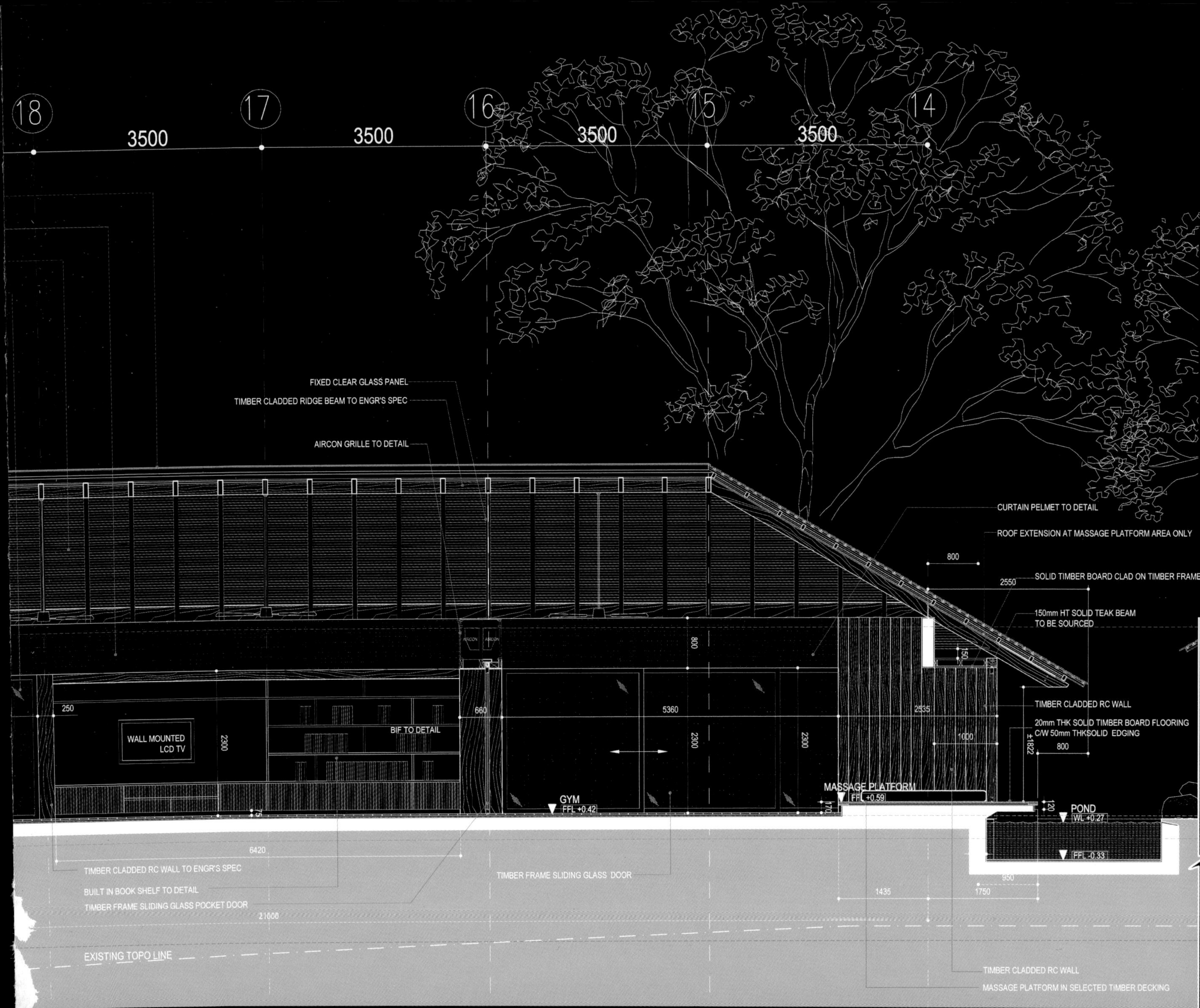

18
17
16
15
14
3500
3500
3500
3500
FIXED CLEAR GLASS PANEL
TIMBER CLADDED RIDGE BEAM TO ENGR'S SPEC
AIRCON GRILLE TO DETAIL
CURTAIN PELMET TO DETAIL
ROOF EXTENSION AT MASSAGE PLATFORM AREA ONLY
800
2550
SOLID TIMBER BOARD CLAD ON TIMBER FRAME
150mm HT SOLID TEAK BEAM
TO BE SOURCED
800
150
TIMBER CLADDED RC WALL
20mm THK SOLID TIMBER BOARD FLOORING
C/W 50mm THKSOLID EDGING
800
±1822
250
WALL MOUNTED
LCD TV
2300
BIF TO DETAIL
660
5360
2300
2300
2535
1000
MASSAGE PLATFORM
FFL +0.59
GYM
FFL +0.42
75
170
120
POND
WL +0.27
FFL -0.33
6420
TIMBER CLADDED RC WALL TO ENGR'S SPEC
BUILT IN BOOK SHELF TO DETAIL
TIMBER FRAME SLIDING GLASS POCKET DOOR
21000
TIMBER FRAME SLIDING GLASS DOOR
950
1435
1750
EXISTING TOPO LINE
TIMBER CLADDED RC WALL
MASSAGE PLATFORM IN SELECTED TIMBER DECKING

ect

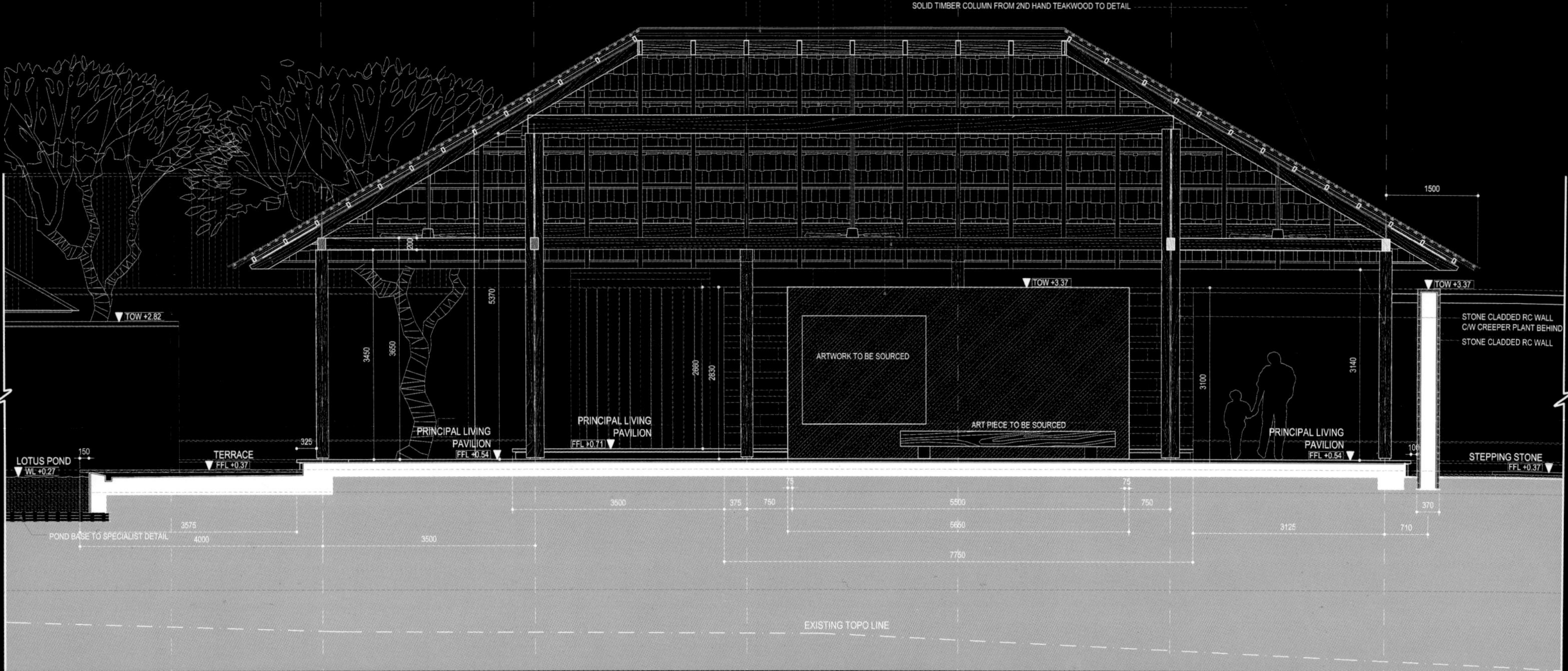
SOLID TIMBER COLUMN FROM 2ND HAND TEAKWOOD TO DETAIL
1500
TOW +3.37
TOW +3.37
TOW +2.82
STONE CLADDED RC WALL C/W CREEPER PLANT BEHIND
STONE CLADDED RC WALL
ARTWORK TO BE SOURCED
ART PIECE TO BE SOURCED
PRINCIPAL LIVING PAVILION
FFL +0.54
PRINCIPAL LIVING PAVILION
FFL +0.71
PRINCIPAL LIVING PAVILION
FFL +0.54
LOTUS POND
WL +0.27
TERRACE
FFL +0.37
STEPPING STONE
FFL +0.37
POND BASE TO SPECIALIST DETAIL
EXISTING TOPO LINE

Interior view of the Main Pavilion.

Detail of structural columns from old recycled wood.

Detail view of different local materials used in the Villa.

Interior view of the Main Pavilion.

Interior view of the Main Pavilion.

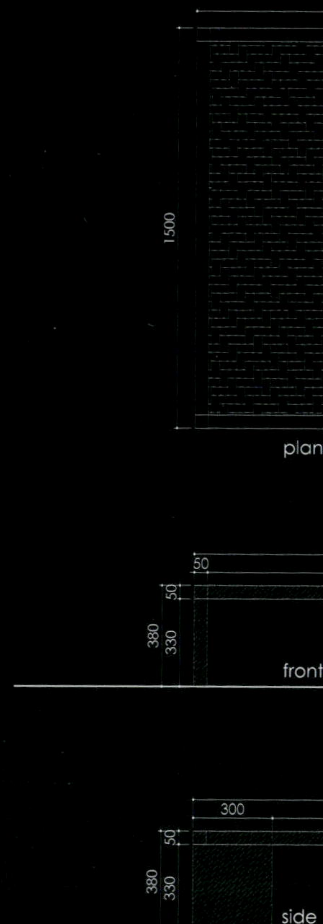

Coffee tables

View of dining area with lamps done made from traditional fishing baskets.

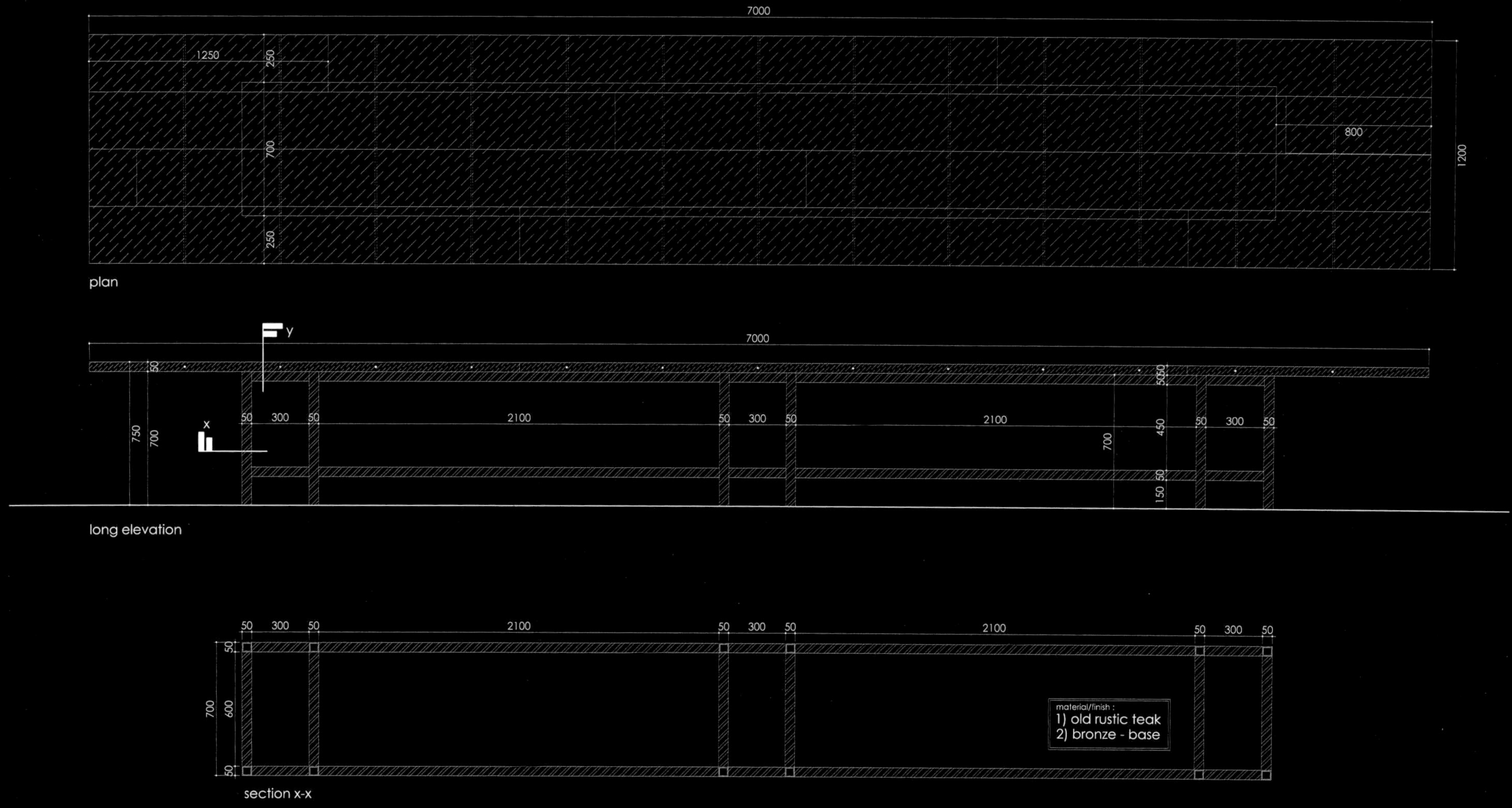

Dining table.

above dining table.

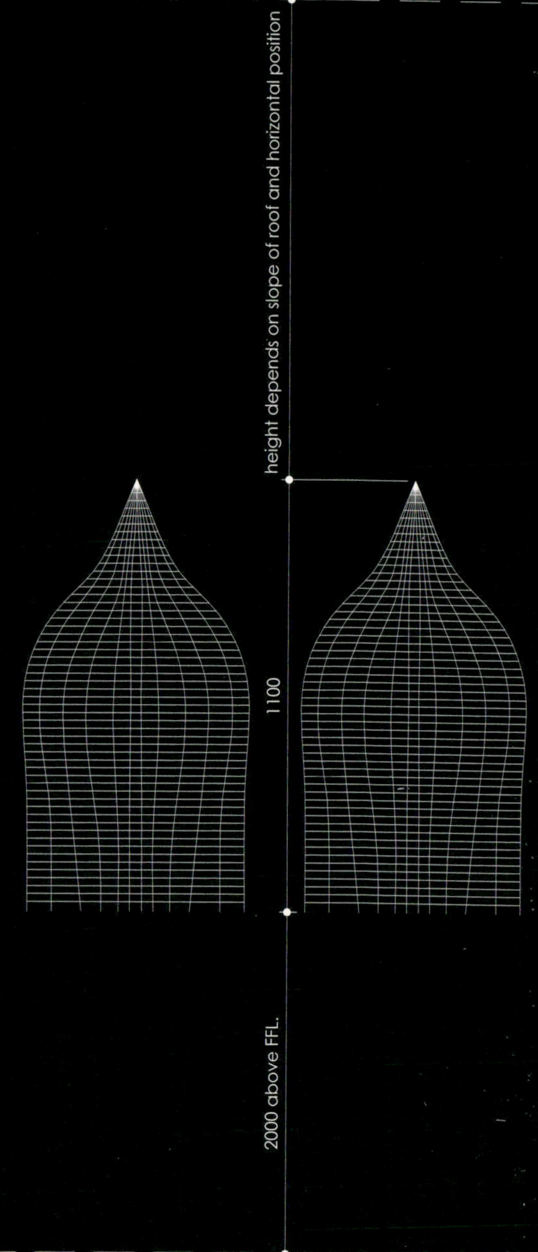

Furniture Details.

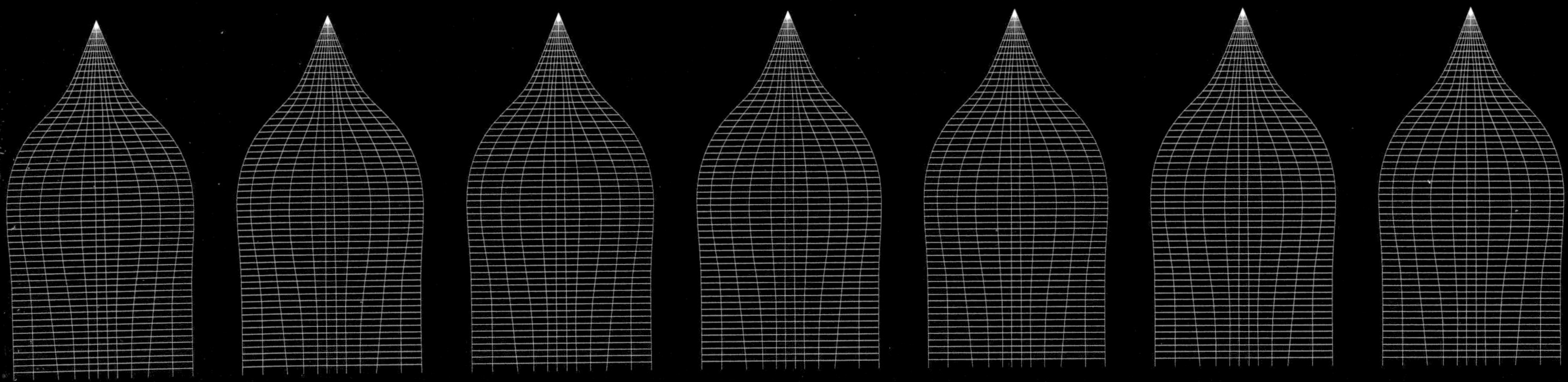

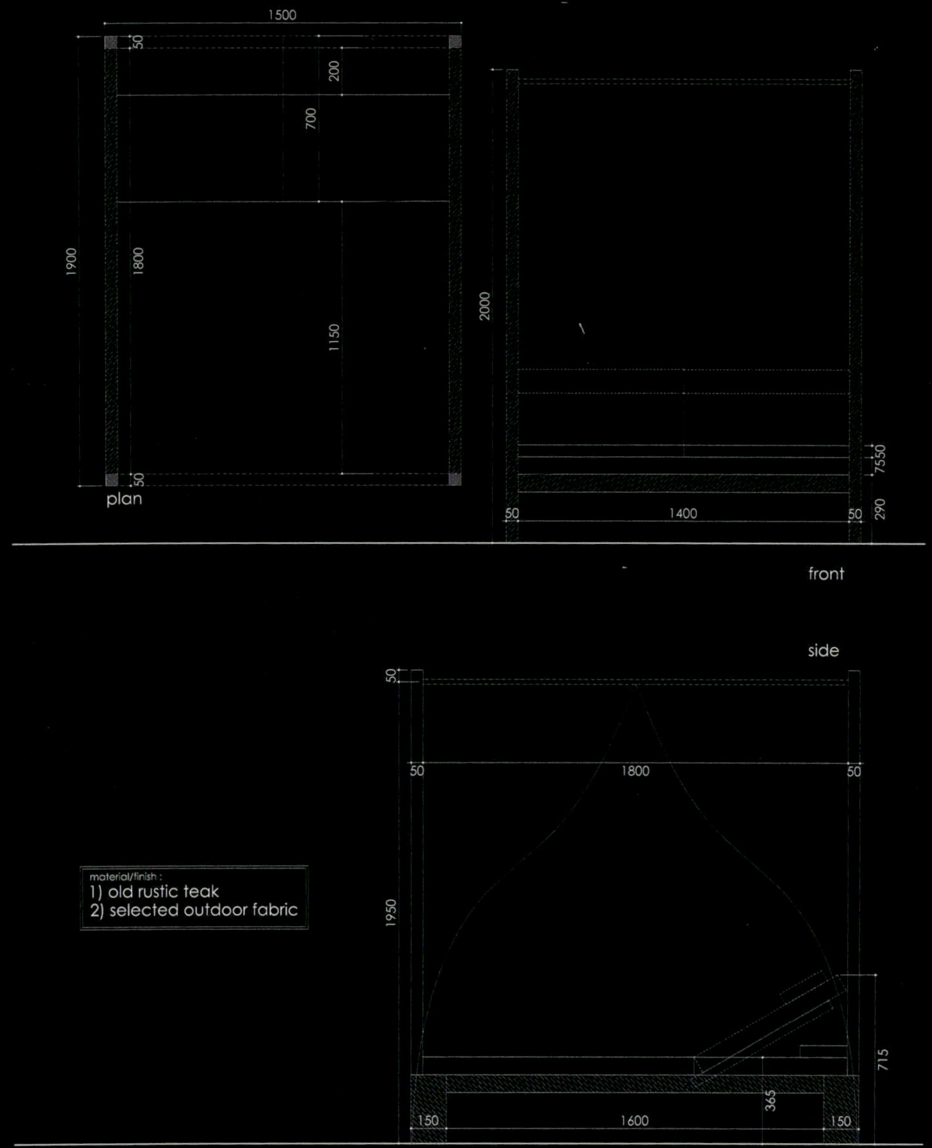

Sun Lounger (double).

View of swimming pool deck with furniture.

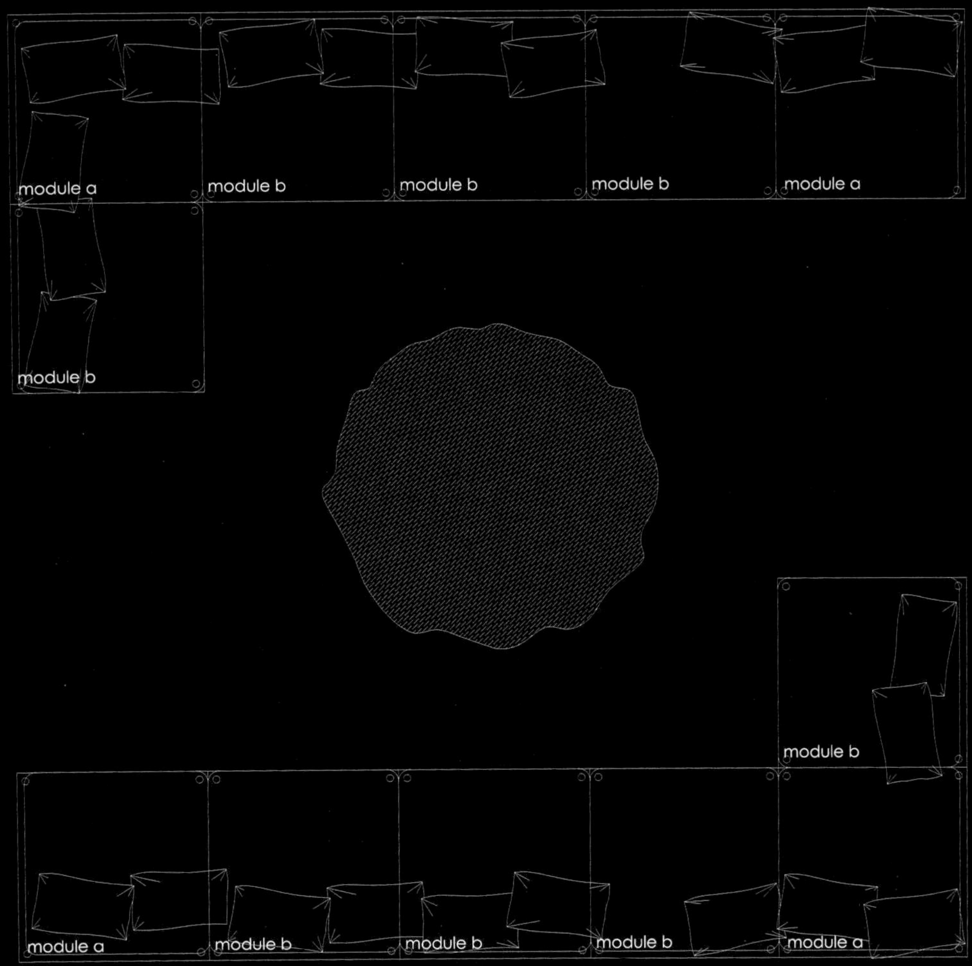

A/B Module.

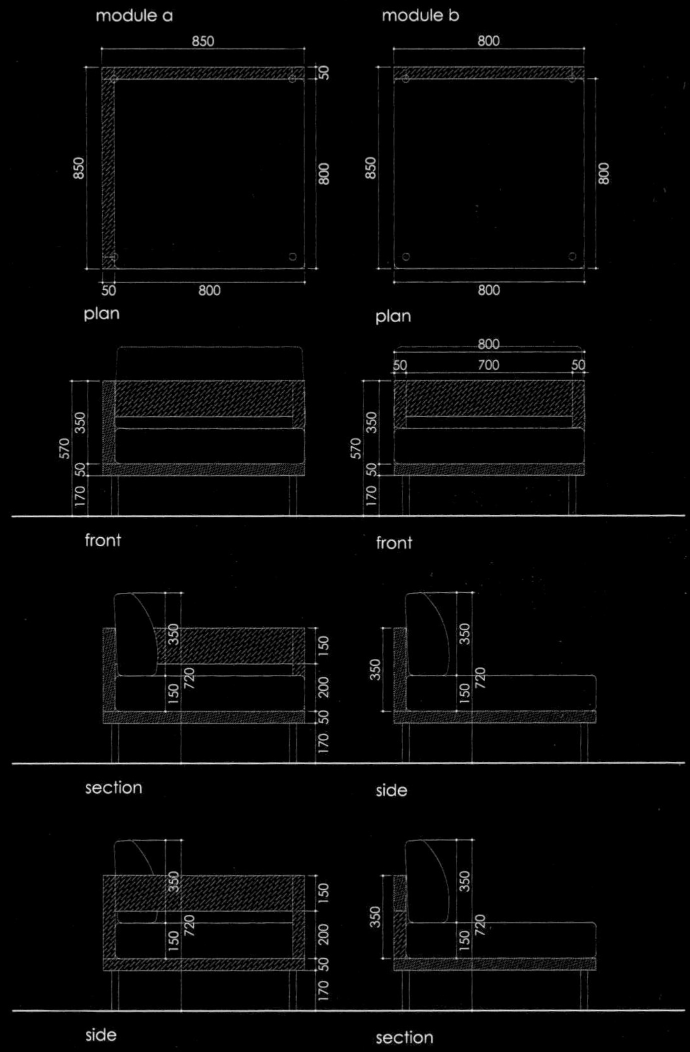

material/finish :
1) old rustic teak
2) selected fabric

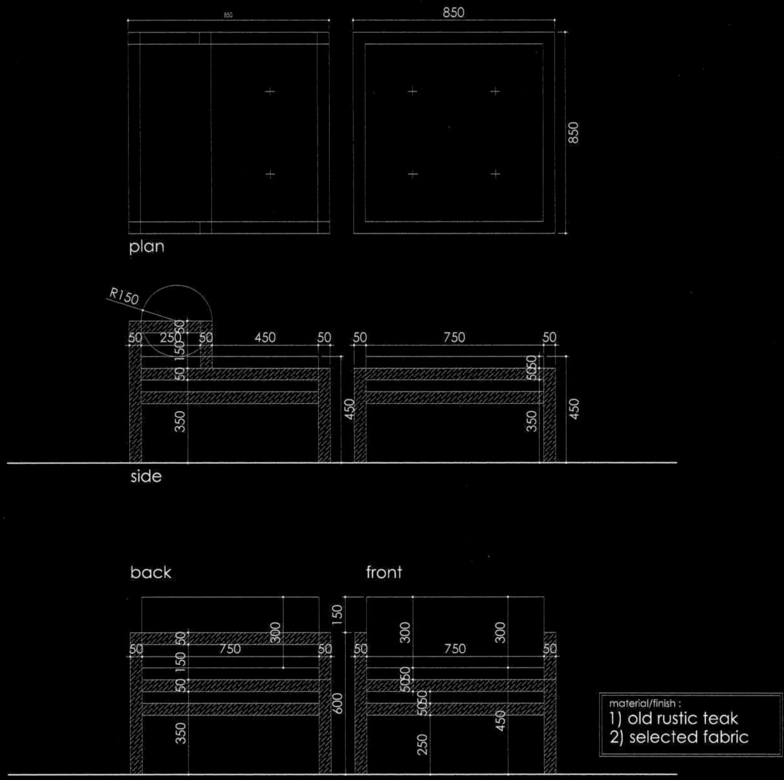

Lounger.

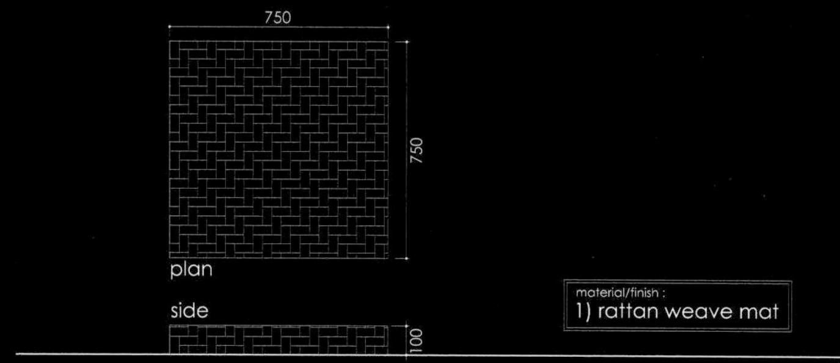

Square Cushion.

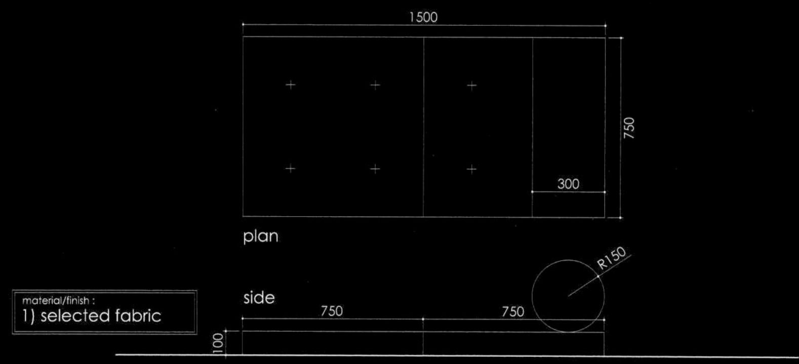

Daybed.

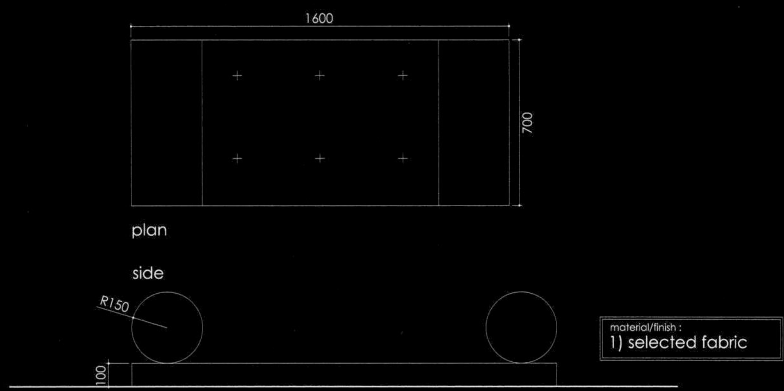

Cushion: Guest 2 & 3.

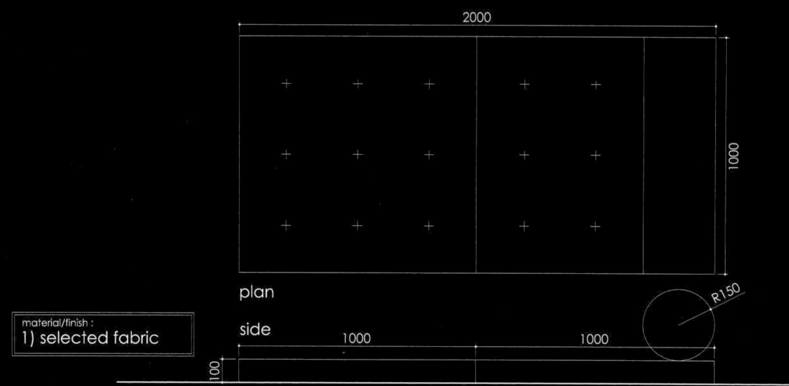

Massage Bed.

View of swimming pool deck with furniture.

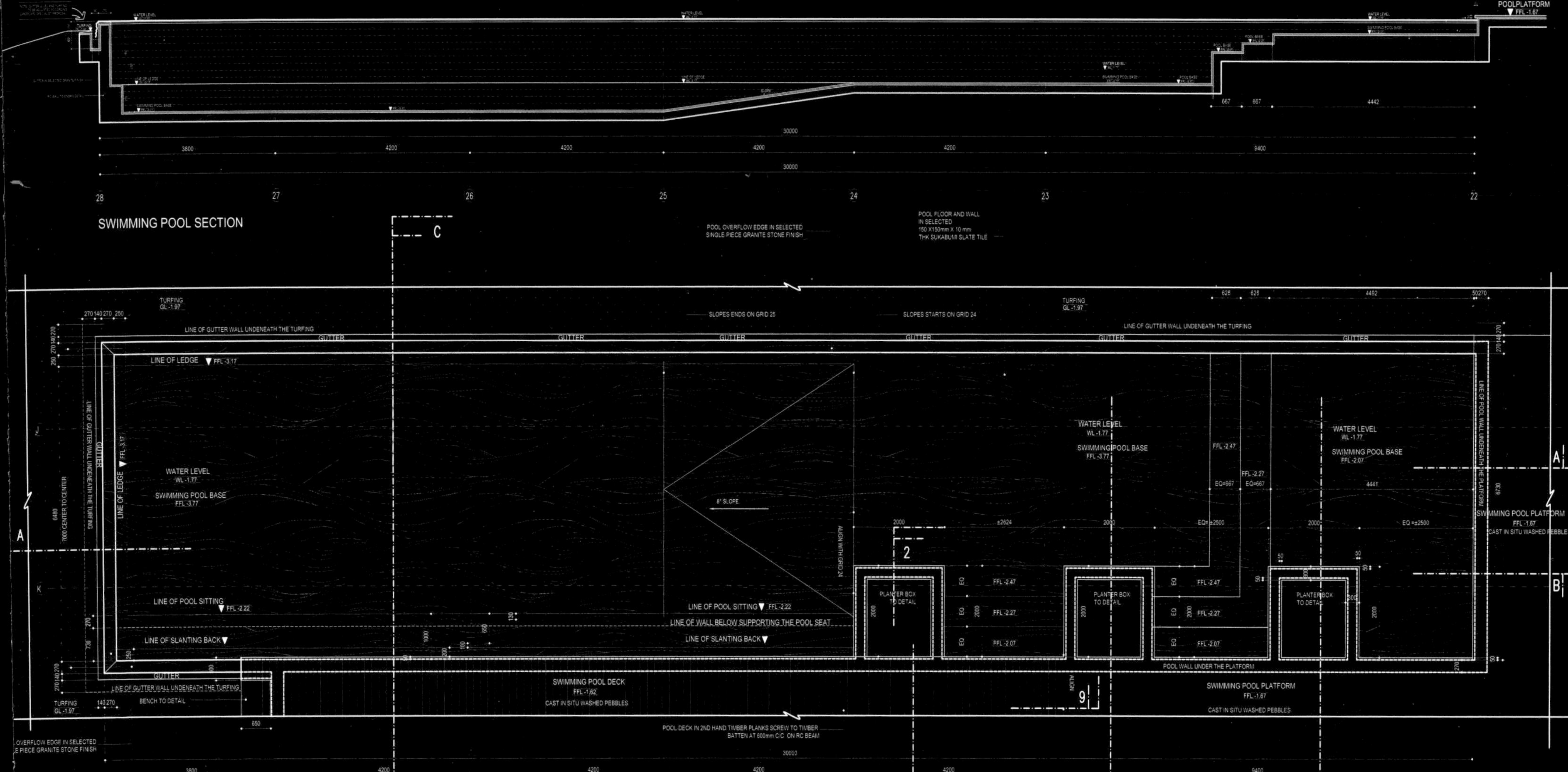

POOLPLATFORM
FFL -1.67
SWIMMING POOL SECTION
POOL OVERFLOW EDGE IN SELECTED SINGLE PIECE GRANITE STONE FINISH
POOL FLOOR AND WALL IN SELECTED 150 X150mm X 10 mm THK SUKABUMI SLATE TILE
TURFING GL -1.97
SLOPES ENDS ON GRID 25
SLOPES STARTS ON GRID 24
LINE OF GUTTER WALL UNDENEATH THE TURFING
GUTTER
LINE OF LEDGE FFL -3.17
WATER LEVEL WL -1.77
SWIMMING POOL BASE FFL -3.77
SWIMMING POOL BASE FFL -2.07
8° SLOPE
LINE OF POOL SITTING FFL -2.22
LINE OF WALL BELOW SUPPORTING THE POOL SEAT
LINE OF SLANTING BACK
ALIGN WITH GRID 24
PLANTER BOX TO DETAIL
FFL -2.47
FFL -2.27
FFL -2.07
LINE OF POOL WALL UNDERNEATH THE PLATFORM
SWIMMING POOL PLATFORM FFL -1.67 CAST IN SITU WASHED PEBBLES
POOL WALL UNDER THE PLATFORM
SWIMMING POOL DECK FFL -1.62 CAST IN SITU WASHED PEBBLES
BENCH TO DETAIL
POOL DECK IN 2ND HAND TIMBER PLANKS SCREW TO TIMBER BATTEN AT 600mm C/C ON RC BEAM
OVERFLOW EDGE IN SELECTED
E PIECE GRANITE STONE FINISH
7000 CENTER TO CENTER
30000
3800
4200
9400
28
27
26
25
24
23
22
A
B
C
2
9

nd.

Project

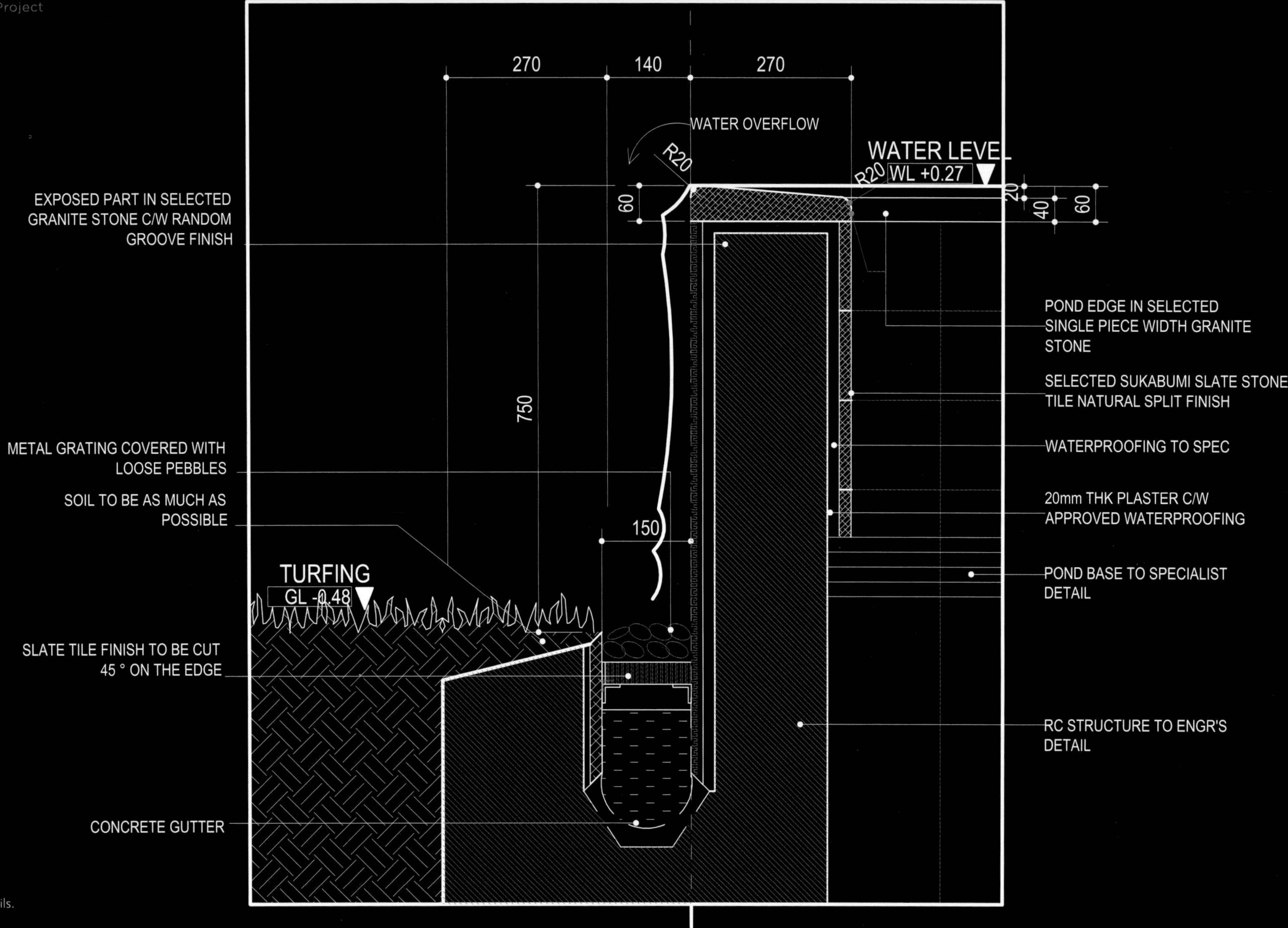

270
140
270
WATER OVERFLOW
R20
WATER LEVEL
R20
WL +0.27
20
40
60
60
EXPOSED PART IN SELECTED GRANITE STONE C/W RANDOM GROOVE FINISH
POND EDGE IN SELECTED SINGLE PIECE WIDTH GRANITE STONE
SELECTED SUKABUMI SLATE STONE TILE NATURAL SPLIT FINISH
750
METAL GRATING COVERED WITH LOOSE PEBBLES
WATERPROOFING TO SPEC
SOIL TO BE AS MUCH AS POSSIBLE
20mm THK PLASTER C/W APPROVED WATERPROOFING
150
TURFING
GL -0.48
POND BASE TO SPECIALIST DETAIL
SLATE TILE FINISH TO BE CUT 45 ° ON THE EDGE
RC STRUCTURE TO ENGR'S DETAIL
CONCRETE GUTTER

ils.

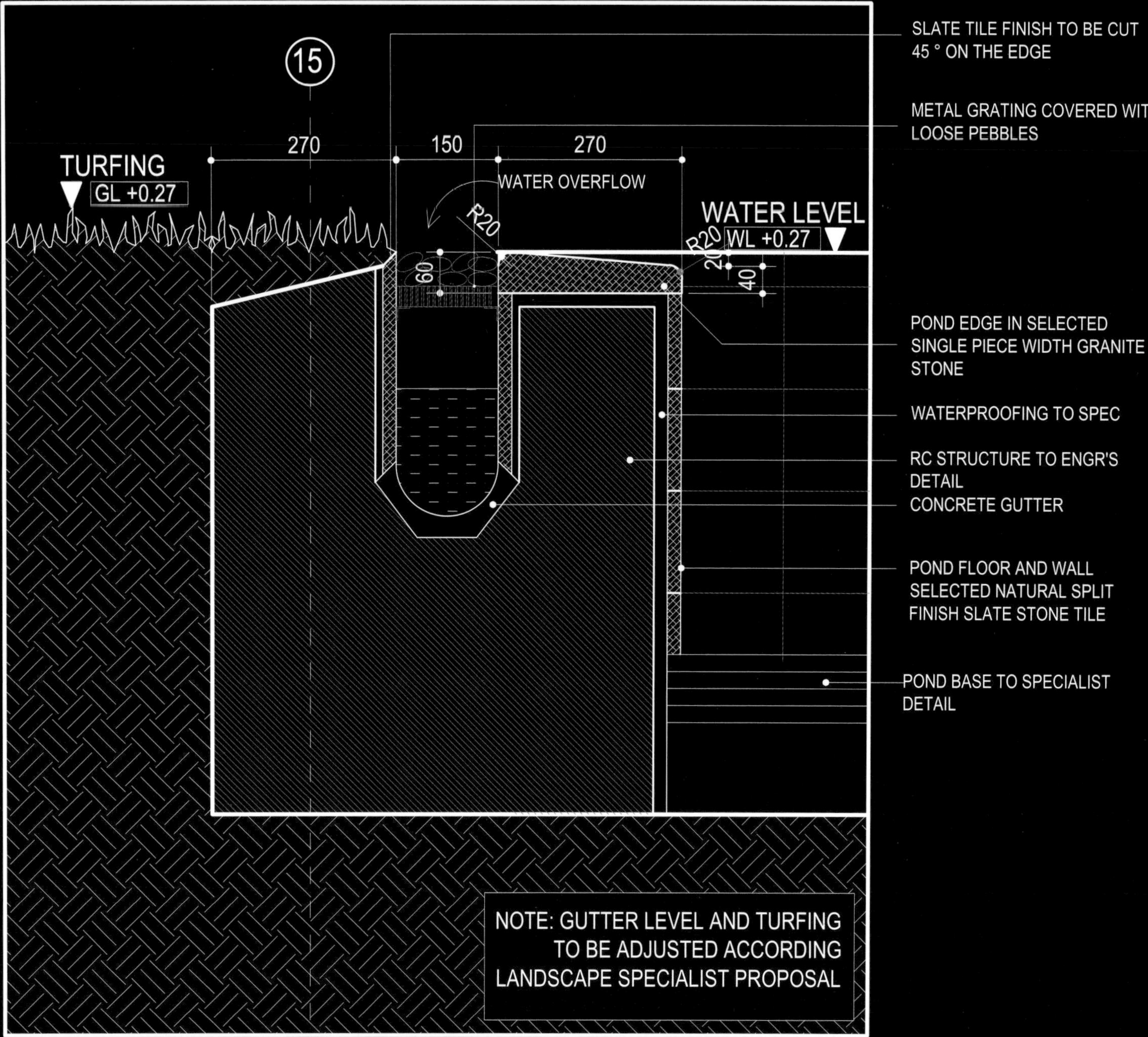
15
270
150
270
TURFING
GL +0.27
WATER OVERFLOW
R20
WATER LEVEL
R20
WL +0.27
60
20
40
SLATE TILE FINISH TO BE CUT
45 ° ON THE EDGE
METAL GRATING COVERED WIT
LOOSE PEBBLES
POND EDGE IN SELECTED
SINGLE PIECE WIDTH GRANITE
STONE
WATERPROOFING TO SPEC
RC STRUCTURE TO ENGR'S
DETAIL
CONCRETE GUTTER
POND FLOOR AND WALL
SELECTED NATURAL SPLIT
FINISH SLATE STONE TILE
POND BASE TO SPECIALIST
DETAIL
NOTE: GUTTER LEVEL AND TURFING
TO BE ADJUSTED ACCORDING
LANDSCAPE SPECIALIST PROPOSAL

Overall view of swimming pool.

View of pond and walls enclosing the private gardens of the

View of link walkway into private Guest Pavilion.

Overall view of 2nd Court with private Guest Villas in the background.

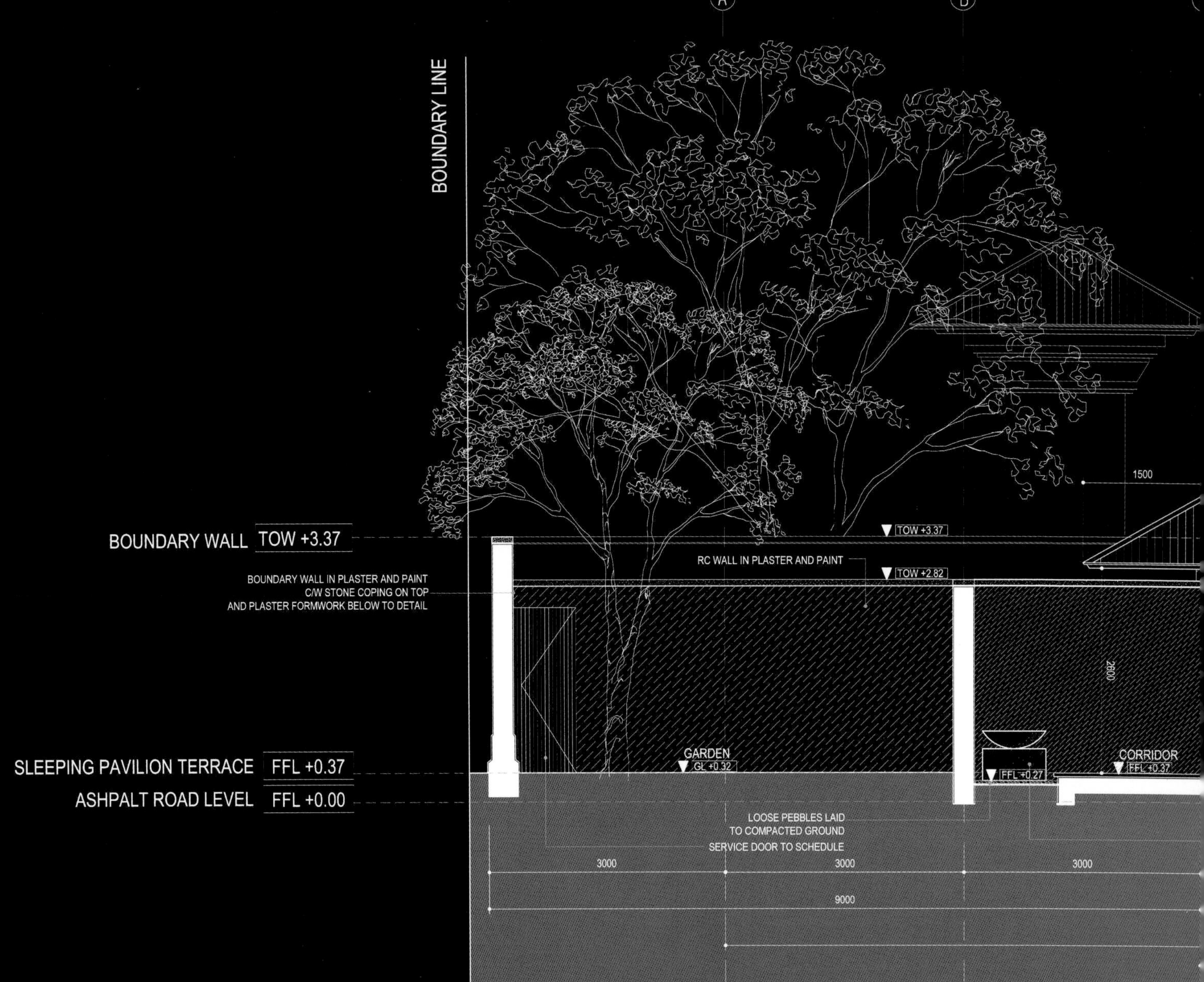

Guest Pavilion Elevation.

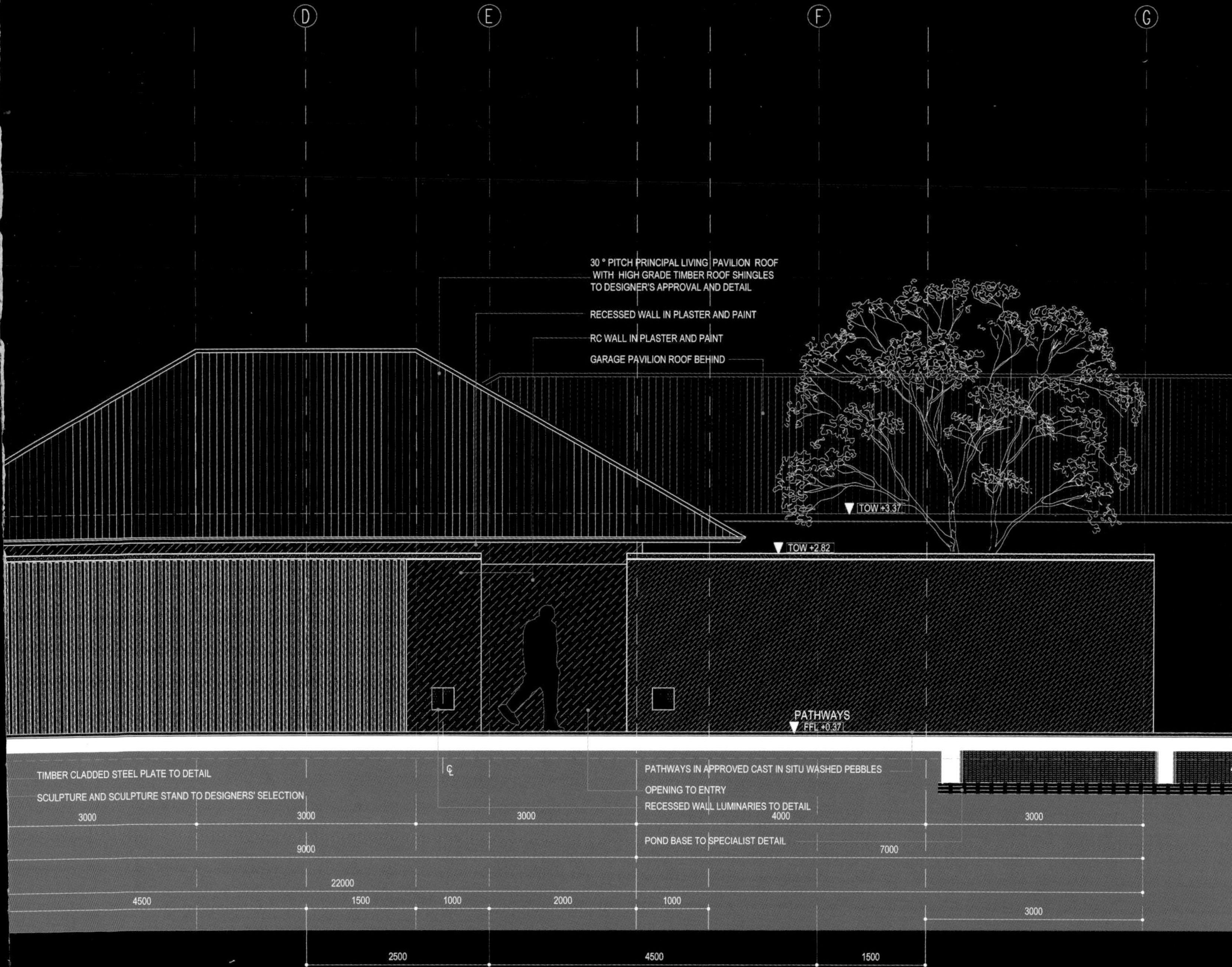

D
E
F
G
30 ° PITCH PRINCIPAL LIVING PAVILION ROOF
WITH HIGH GRADE TIMBER ROOF SHINGLES
TO DESIGNER'S APPROVAL AND DETAIL
RECESSED WALL IN PLASTER AND PAINT
RC WALL IN PLASTER AND PAINT
GARAGE PAVILION ROOF BEHIND
TOW +3.37
TOW +2.82
PATHWAYS
FFL +0.37
TIMBER CLADDED STEEL PLATE TO DETAIL
SCULPTURE AND SCULPTURE STAND TO DESIGNERS' SELECTION
PATHWAYS IN APPROVED CAST IN SITU WASHED PEBBLES
OPENING TO ENTRY
RECESSED WALL LUMINARIES TO DETAIL
POND BASE TO SPECIALIST DETAIL
3000
3000
3000
4000
3000
9000
7000
22000
4500
1500
1000
2000
1000
3000
2500
4500
1500

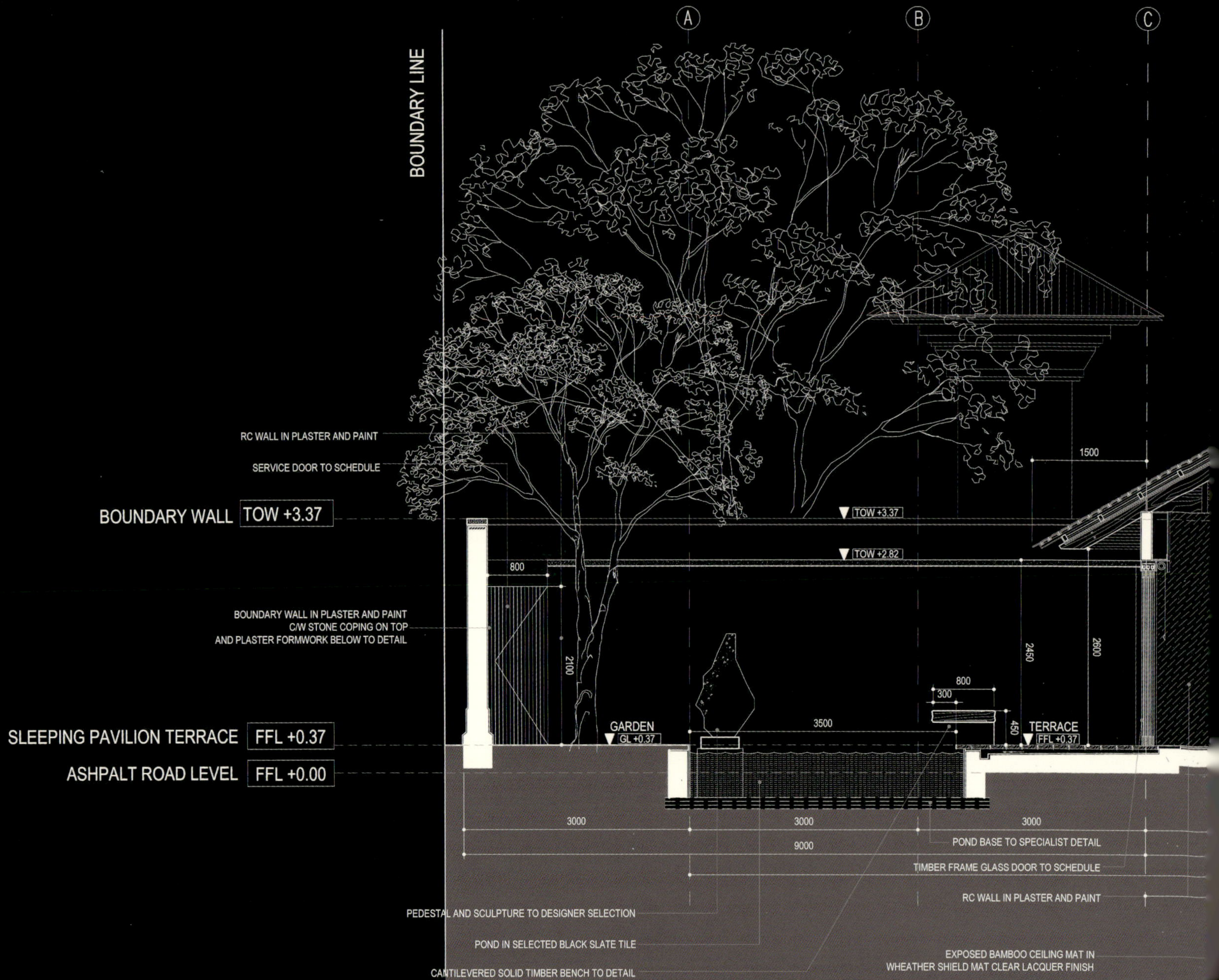

Guest Pavilion Section.

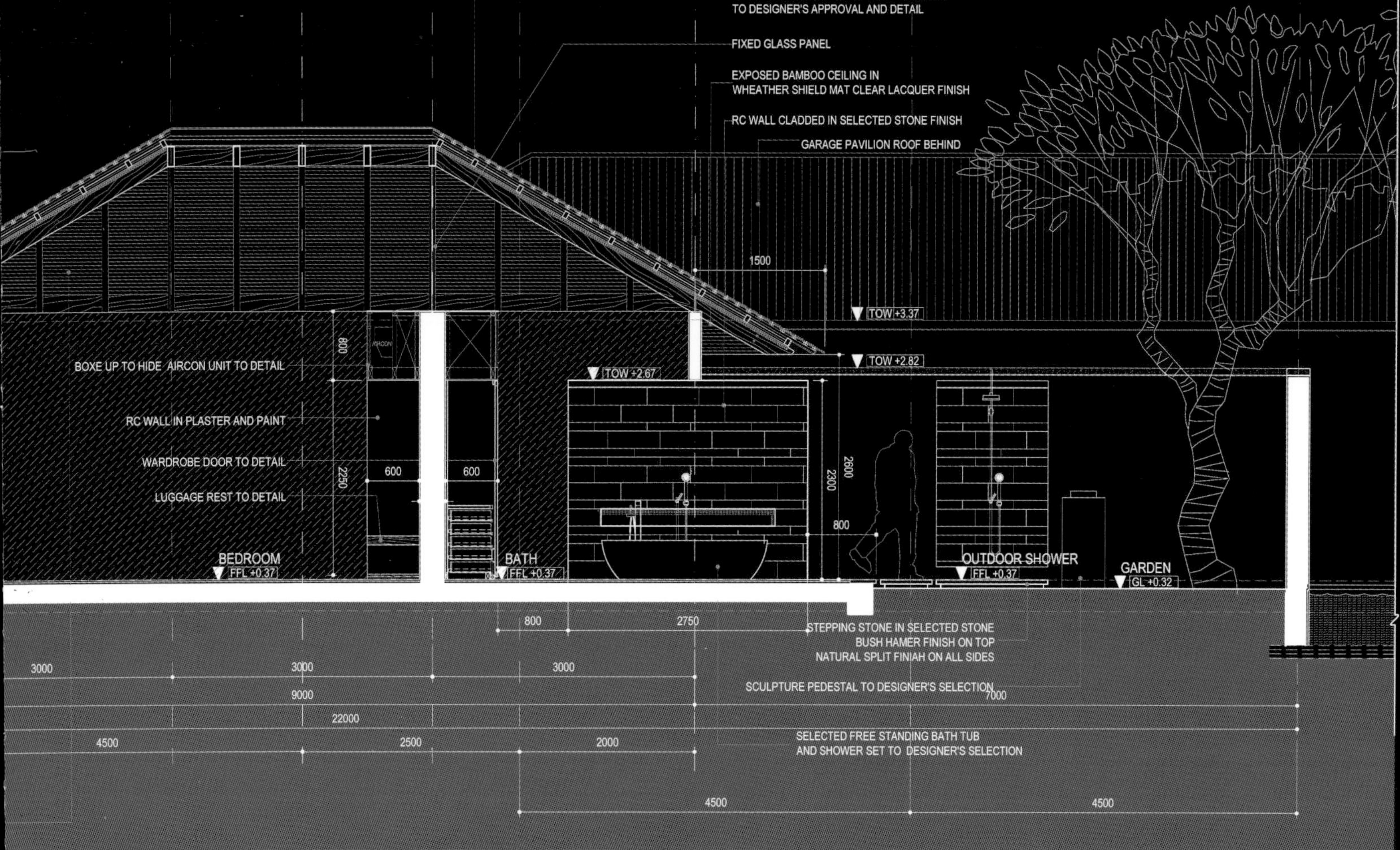

TO DESIGNER'S APPROVAL AND DETAIL
FIXED GLASS PANEL
EXPOSED BAMBOO CEILING IN
WHEATHER SHIELD MAT CLEAR LACQUER FINISH
RC WALL CLADDED IN SELECTED STONE FINISH
GARAGE PAVILION ROOF BEHIND
1500
TOW +3.37
TOW +2.82
TOW +2.67
800
AIRCON
BOXE UP TO HIDE AIRCON UNIT TO DETAIL
RC WALL IN PLASTER AND PAINT
WARDROBE DOOR TO DETAIL
LUGGAGE REST TO DETAIL
2250
600
600
2600
2300
800
BEDROOM
FFL +0.37
BATH
FFL +0.37
OUTDOOR SHOWER
FFL +0.37
GARDEN
GL +0.32
800
2750
STEPPING STONE IN SELECTED STONE
BUSH HAMER FINISH ON TOP
NATURAL SPLIT FINIAH ON ALL SIDES
3000
3000
3000
SCULPTURE PEDESTAL TO DESIGNER'S SELECTION
9000
7000
22000
SELECTED FREE STANDING BATH TUB
AND SHOWER SET TO DESIGNER'S SELECTION
4500
2500
2000
4500
4500

View of internal 3rd Court inside the Guest Villa; stone garden, circulation, and timber screens.

ew of internal ard Court inside the Guest Villa: stone garden, circulation, and timber screens

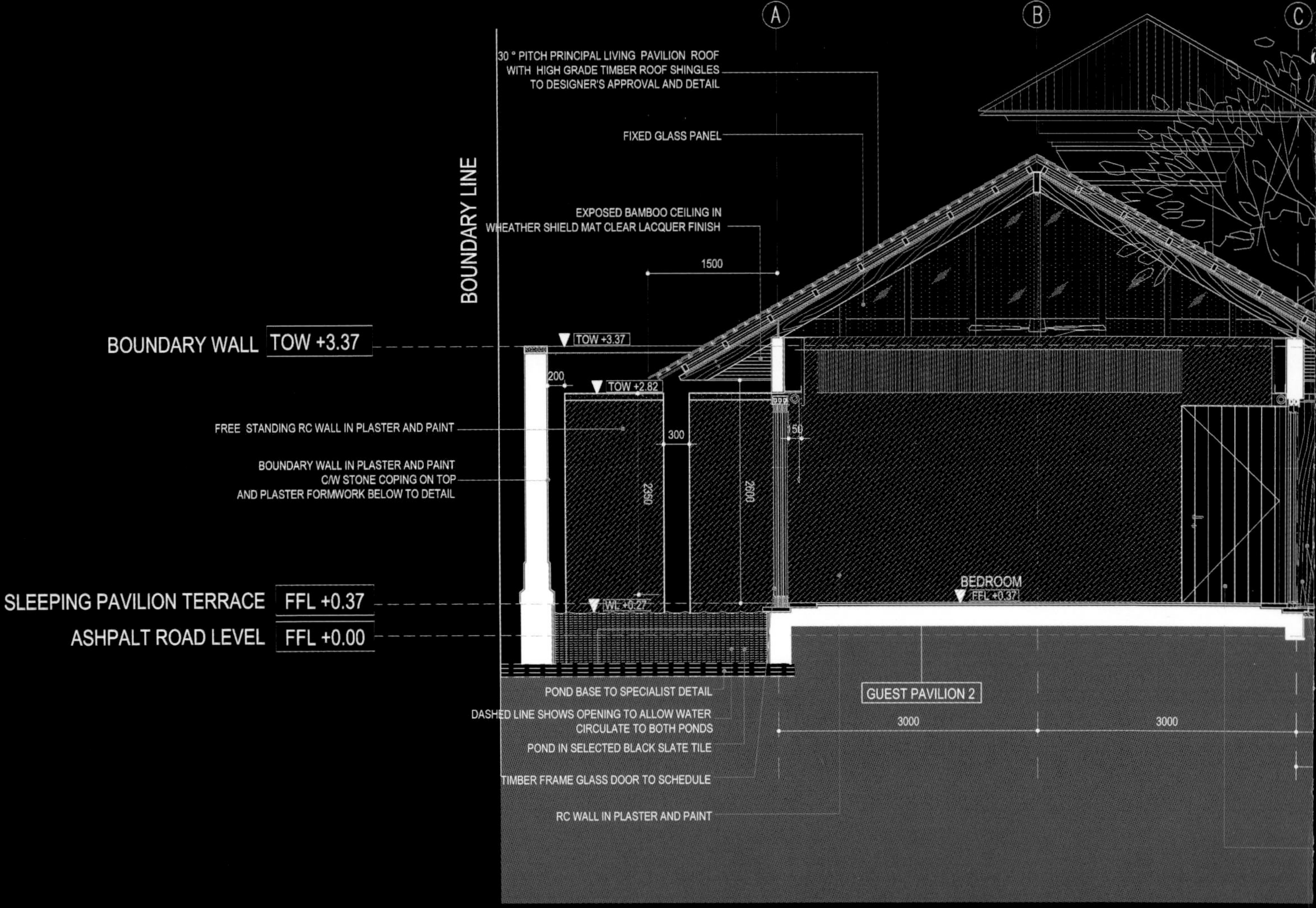

Guest Pavilion Section.

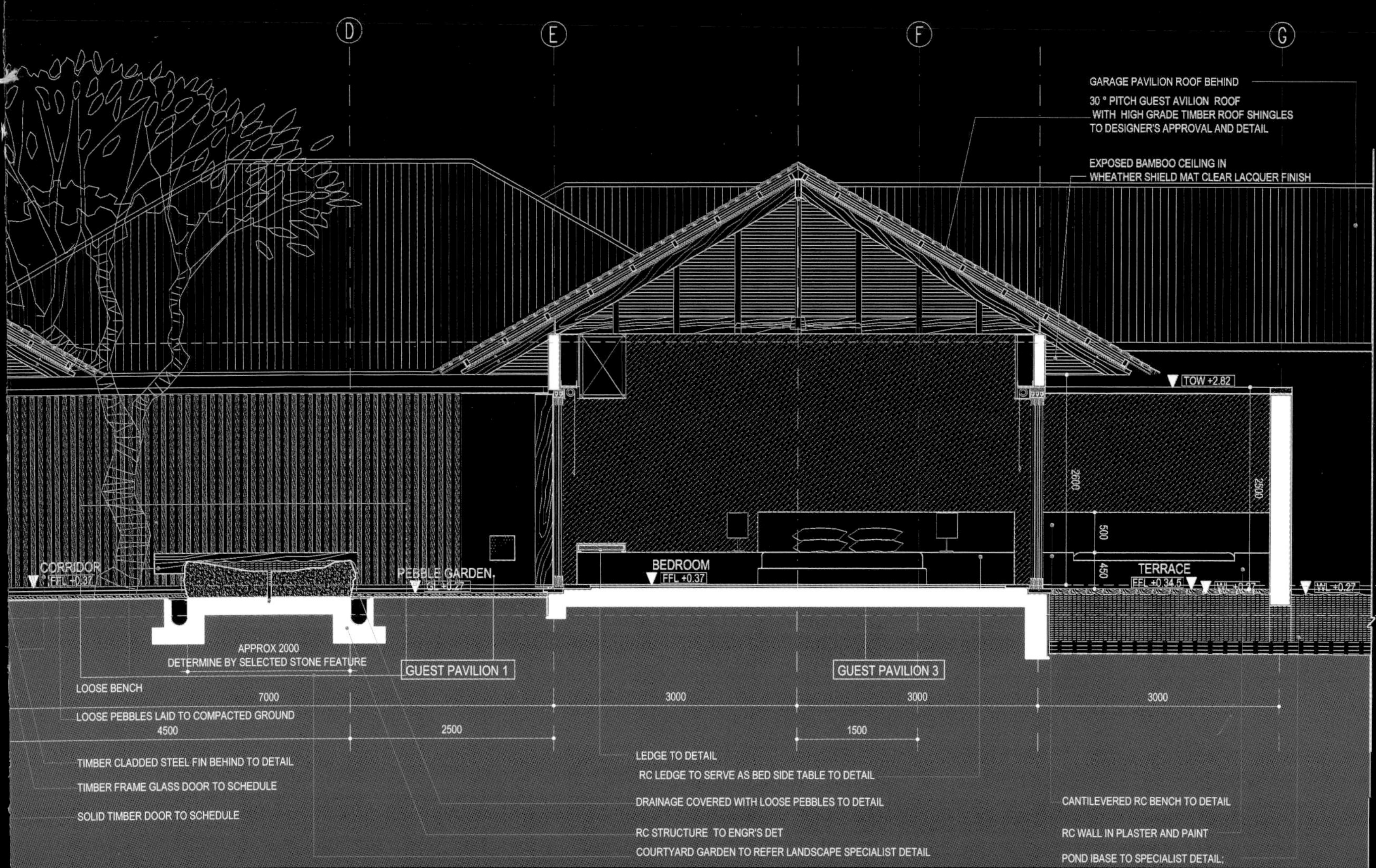

D
E
F
G
GARAGE PAVILION ROOF BEHIND
30 ° PITCH GUEST AVILION ROOF
WITH HIGH GRADE TIMBER ROOF SHINGLES
TO DESIGNER'S APPROVAL AND DETAIL
EXPOSED BAMBOO CEILING IN
WHEATHER SHIELD MAT CLEAR LACQUER FINISH
TOW +2.82
2600
2500
500
450
CORRIDOR
FFL +0.37
PEBBLE GARDEN
GL +0.27
BEDROOM
FFL +0.37
TERRACE
FFL +0.34.5
WL +0.37
WL +0.27
APPROX 2000
DETERMINE BY SELECTED STONE FEATURE
GUEST PAVILION 1
GUEST PAVILION 3
LOOSE BENCH
7000
3000
3000
3000
LOOSE PEBBLES LAID TO COMPACTED GROUND
4500
2500
1500
TIMBER CLADDED STEEL FIN BEHIND TO DETAIL
TIMBER FRAME GLASS DOOR TO SCHEDULE
SOLID TIMBER DOOR TO SCHEDULE
LEDGE TO DETAIL
RC LEDGE TO SERVE AS BED SIDE TABLE TO DETAIL
DRAINAGE COVERED WITH LOOSE PEBBLES TO DETAIL
RC STRUCTURE TO ENGR'S DET
COURTYARD GARDEN TO REFER LANDSCAPE SPECIALIST DETAIL
CANTILEVERED RC BENCH TO DETAIL
RC WALL IN PLASTER AND PAINT
POND IBASE TO SPECIALIST DETAIL;

Guest Pavilion Section.

8A
9A
10
10A
12A
TOW +3.37
RC BEAM IN PLASTER AND PAINT FINISH
PLASTER AND PAINT CURTAIN PELMET TO DETAIL
TIMBER CLADDED STEEL PLATE TO DETAIL
TIMBER FRAME SLIDING DOOR TO SCHEDULE
2300
PEBBLES GARDEN
GL +0.27
PATHWAY
FFL +0.37
BATHROOM
FFL +0.37
GARDEN
GL +0.32
APPROX 3000
DETERMINED BY SELECTED STONE FEATURE
2000
750
750
1500
3000
1500
SOLID STONE WATER FEATURE TO DESIGNER'S SELECTION
GUEST PAVILION 4
WARDROBE TO DETAIL
RC STRUCTURE TO SUPPORT STONE FEATURE TO ENGR'S SPEC
DRAINAGE COVERED WITH LOOSE PEBBLES TO DETAIL
TIMBER STRIP PANEL TO DETAIL
TIMBER FRAME GLASS DOOR TO SCHEDULE
3000
3000
3500
6000
LOOSE TIMBER BENCH TO BE SOURCED
COURTYARD GARDEN TO REFER LANDSCAPE SPECIALIST DETAIL
TIMBER CLADDED STEEL PLATE TO DETAIL

View of internal 3rd Court inside the Guest Villa; stone garden, circulation, and timber screens.

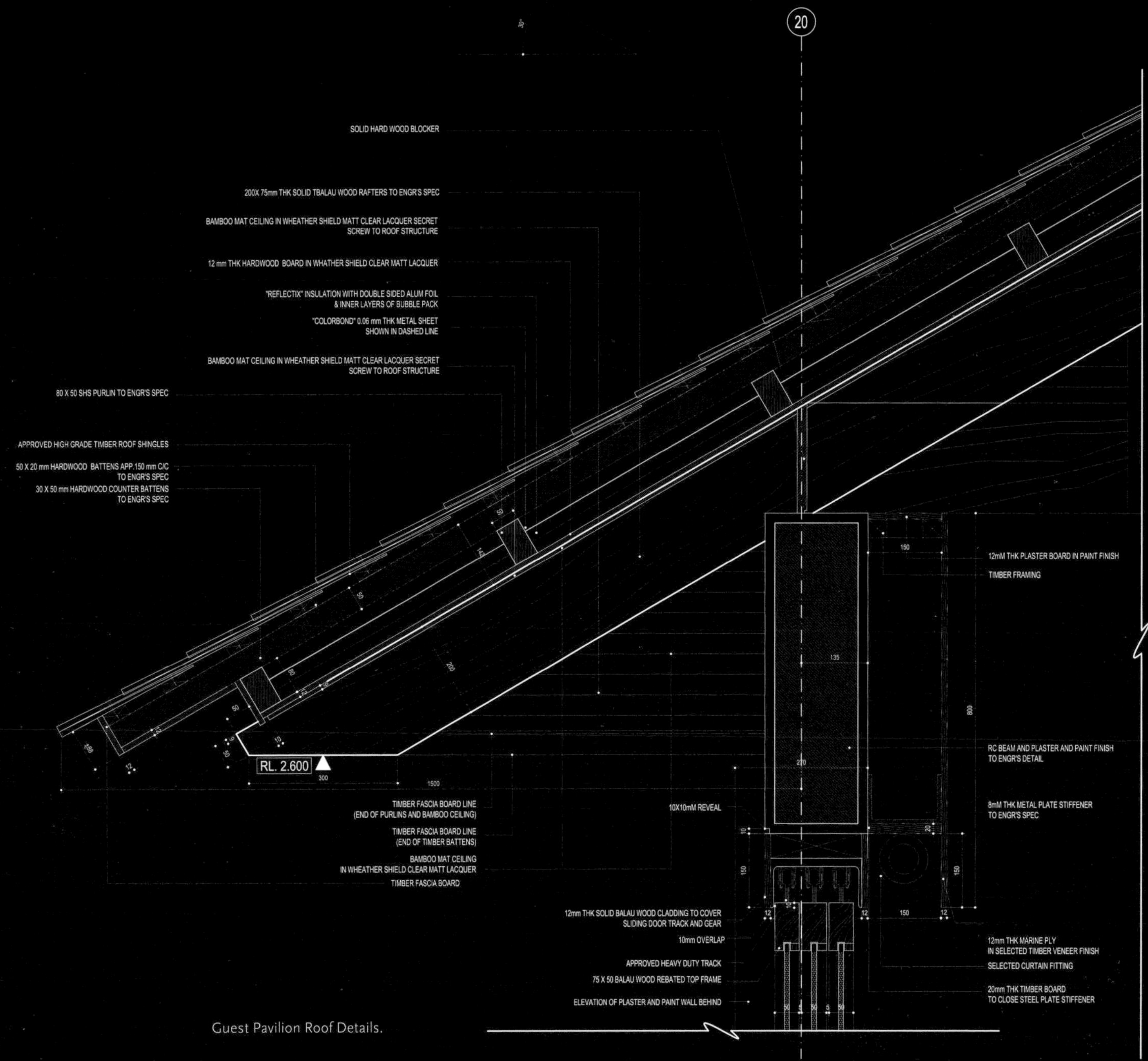

Guest Pavilion Roof Details.

View of internal 3rd Court inside the Guest Villa; stone garden, circulation, and timber screens.

View of circulation into private Guest Villas.

w of internal ard Court inside the Guest Villa: stone garden, circulation, and timber screens.

Overall view of one of the private Guest Villas.

Overall view of one of the private Guest Villas.

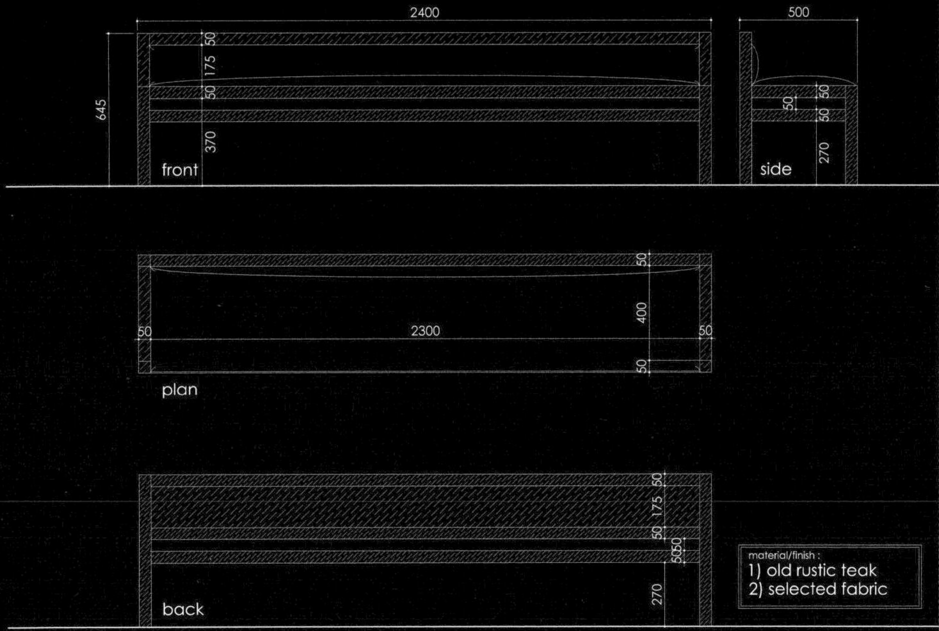

Dining Bench.

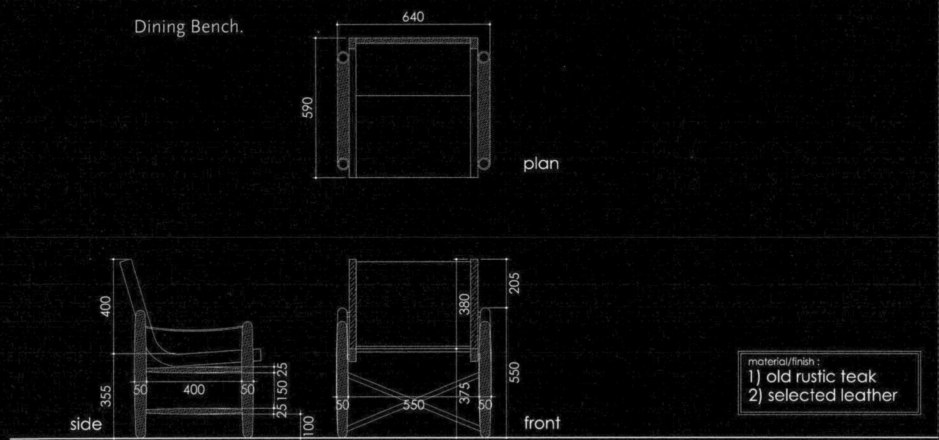

Low Folding Chair.

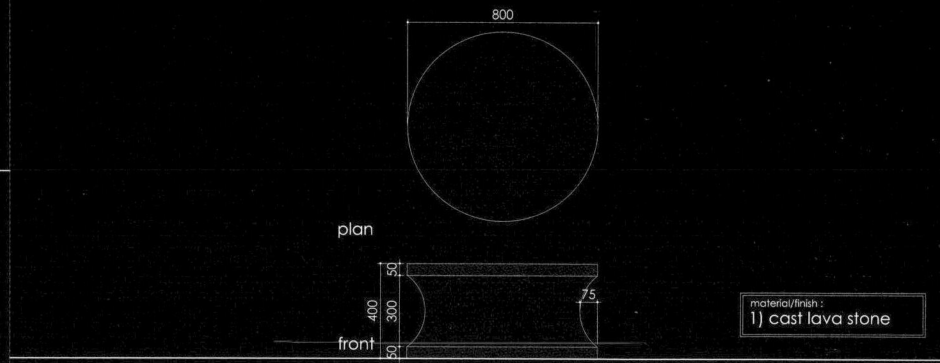

Stone Table.

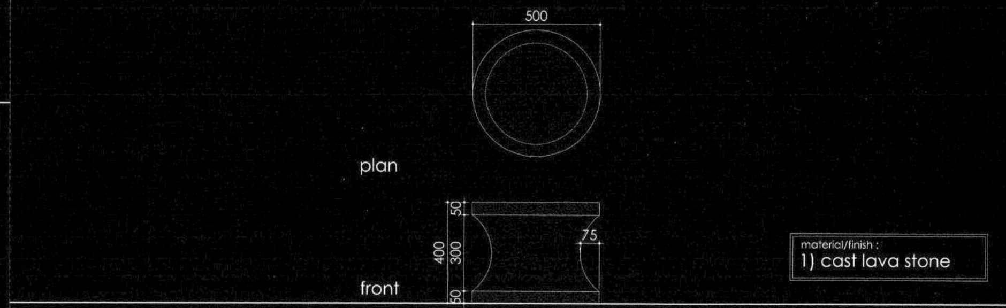

Stone Table.

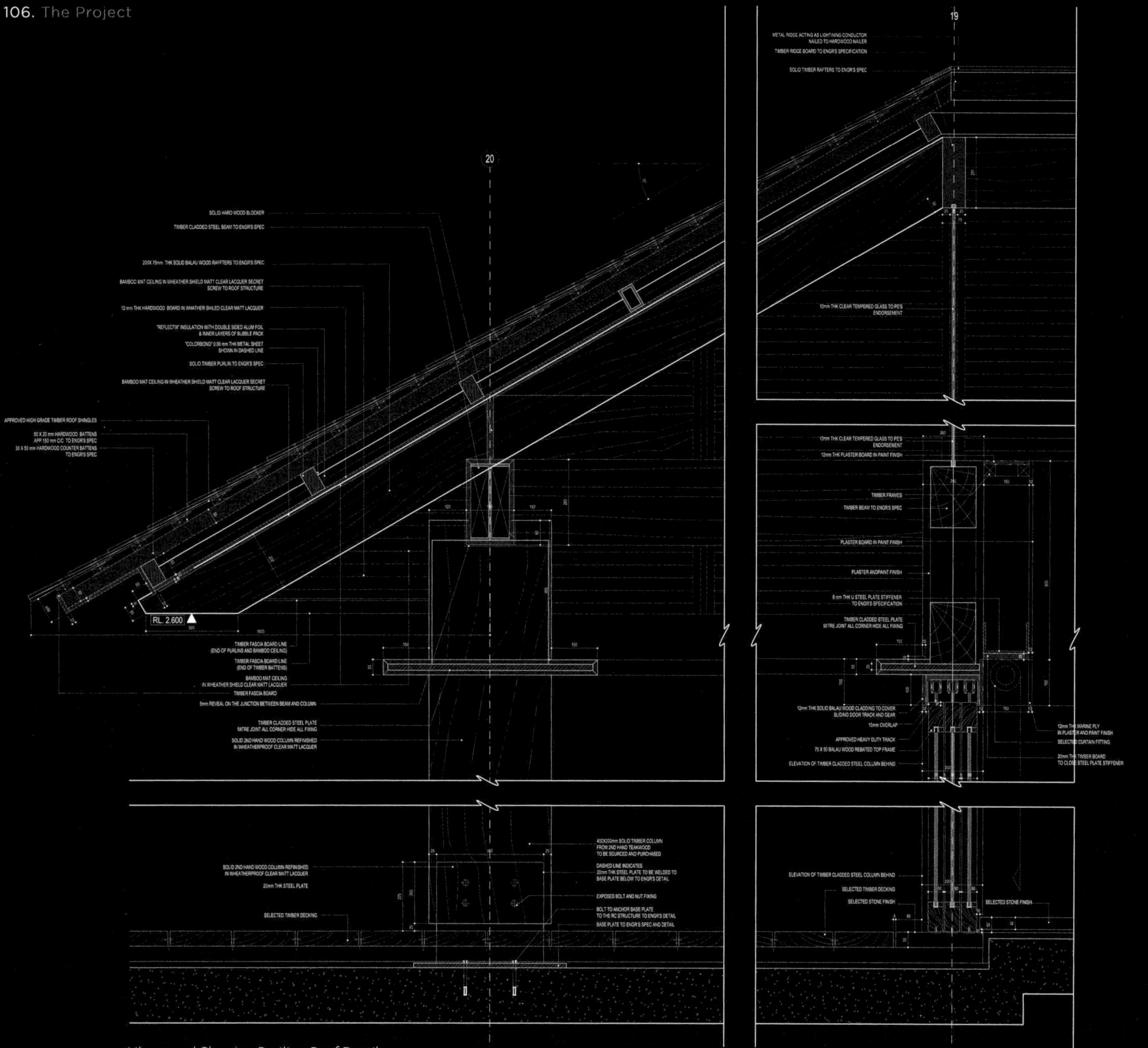

Library and Sleeping Pavilion Roof Details.

General view of Guest Villa interior.

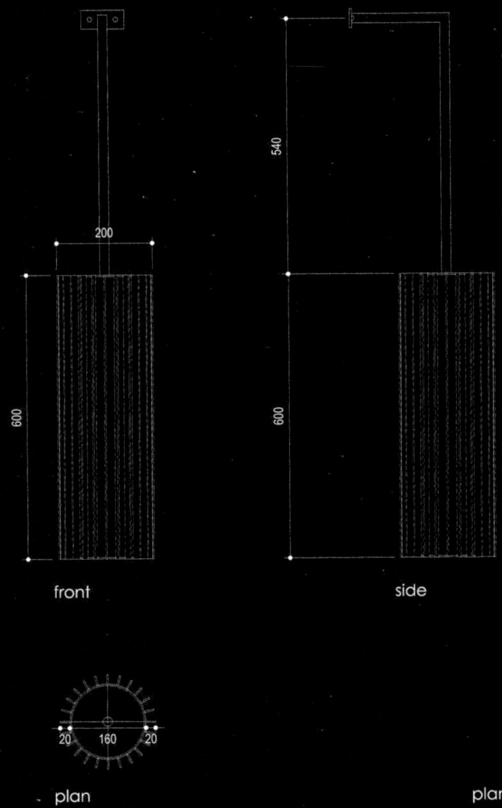

Pendant Lamp.

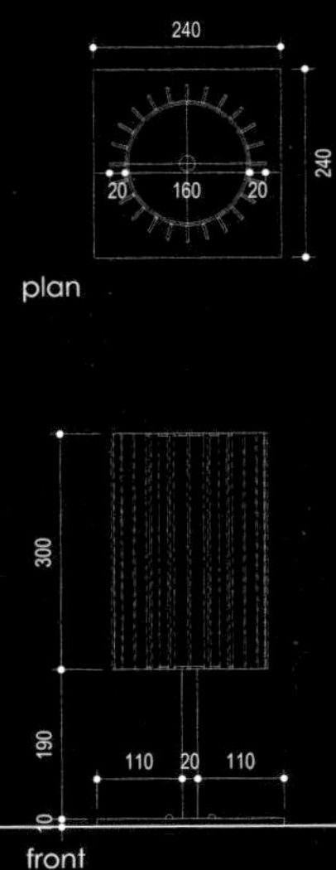

Table Lamp.

material/finish :
1) 3mm THK bronze plate
2) acrylic

Small Lantern.

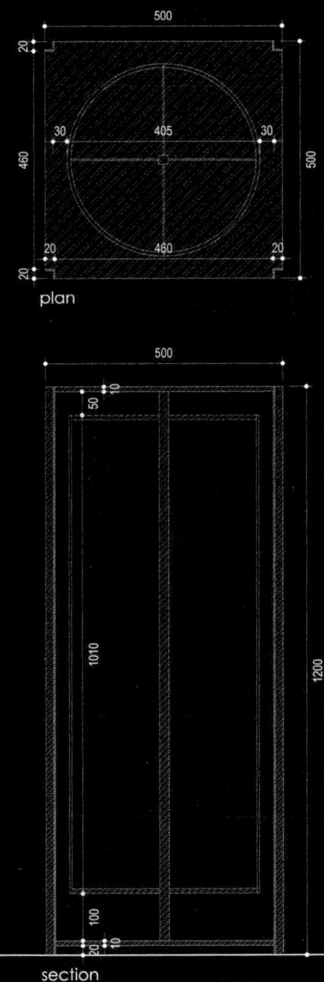

Large Lantern.

Detail view of furniture built in situ & outdoor stone table designed by Ernesto Bedmar.

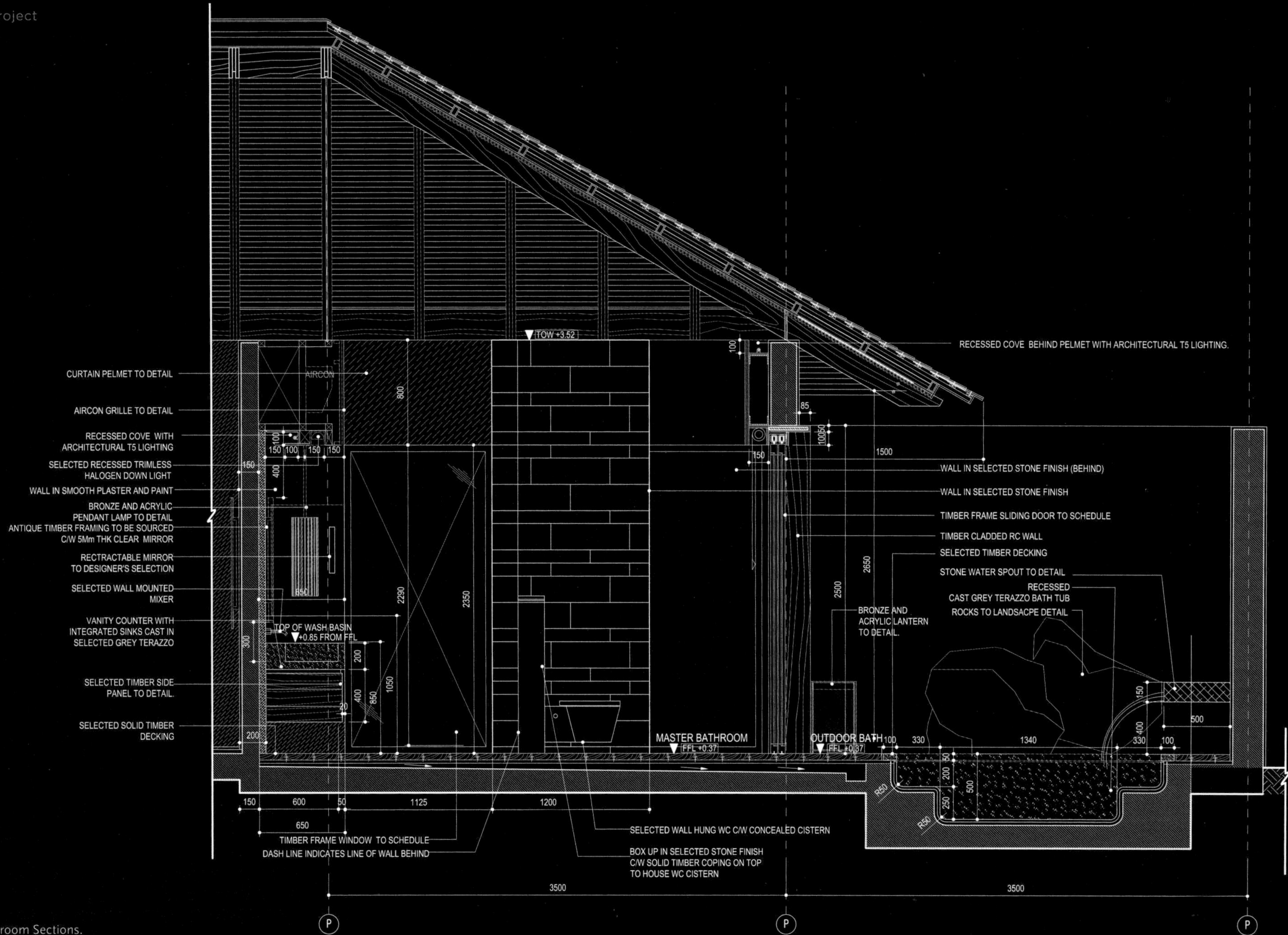

Master Bathroom Sections.

AIRCON
TIMBER CLADDING ON RC WALL
RC WALLL IN SELECTED STONE FINISH
10mm THK FRAMELESS FIXED CLEAR GLASS
BRONZE AND ACRYLIC PENDANT LAMP TO DETAIL
TIMBER FRAME GLASS WINDOW TO SCHEDULE
MIRROR C/W ANTIQUE TIMBER FRAME TO BE SOURCED
SELECTED COMPLETE SET OF SHOWER MIXER
SELECTED COMPLETE HAND SHOWER SET C/W RAIN SHOWER ABOVE
RC WALLL IN SELECTED STONE FINISH
SELECTED TIMBER DOOR PANEL TO DETAIL.
LOTUS POND
WL +0.27
MASTER BATHROOM
WL +0.37
MASTER BATHROOM
WL +0.37
DRAWER
DRAWER
DRAWER
DRAWER
1850
AIRCON GRILLE TO DETAIL
RC WALLL IN SELECTED STONE FINISH
TIMBER CLADDING ON RC WALL
TIMBER FIXED GLASS
RECTRACTABLE MIRROR TO DESIGNER'S SELECTION
10mm THK FRAMELESS FIXED CLEAR GLASS
LEDGE IN 40mm THK SOLID TIMBER
WALL MOUNTED CISTREN ACTUATOR
BOX UP IN SELECTED STONE FINISH
SELECTED PAPER ROLL HOLDER
WALL HUNG WC C/W CONCEALED CISTERN TO DESIGNER'S SELECTION
1540
250
400
2250
400
250
1540
3550
7000
WALL CLADED IN STONE TO DETAIL
SELECTED TIMBER DECKING TO PROVIDE DRAINAGE UNDERNEATH
FLOOR IN SELECTED GREY PEBBLE WASH
SCUPPER DRAIN ALL ARROUND
P
O

Shadow play created by the timber screen in the private Guest Villa facing the stone court.

Detail of hanging bed light designed by Ernesto Bedmar.

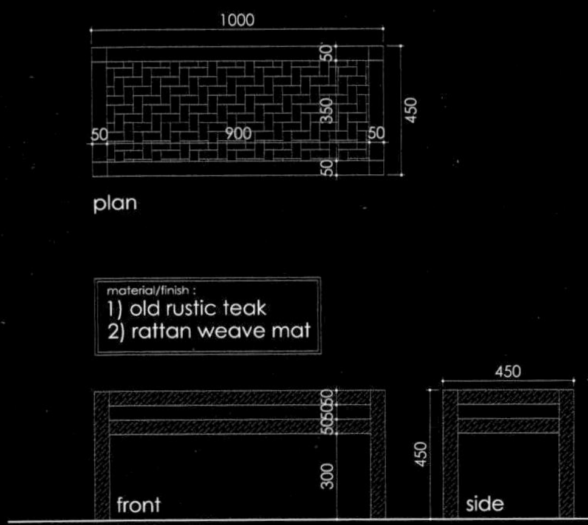

Bench.

Stool.

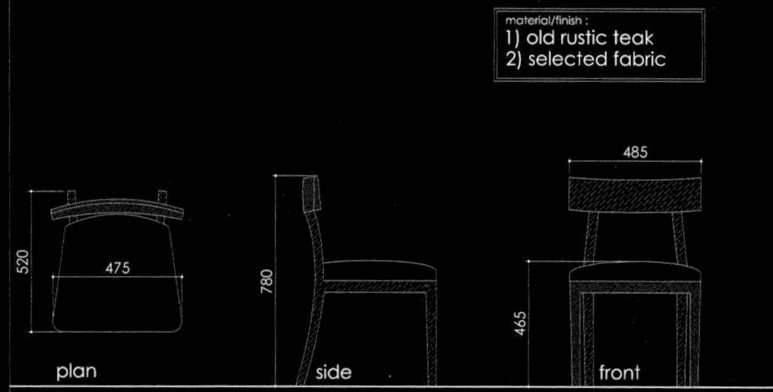

Dining Chair.

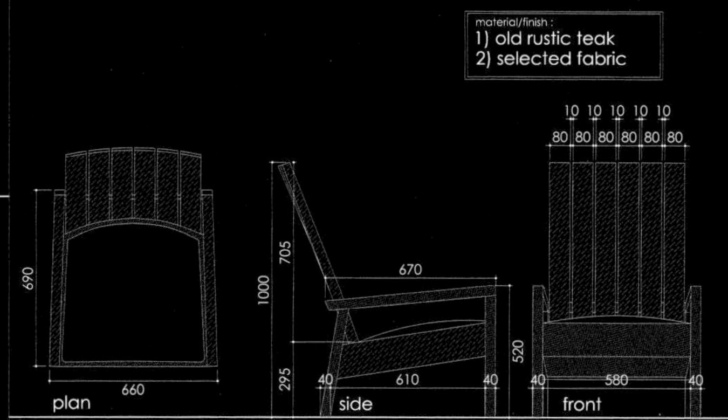

Aron Chair.

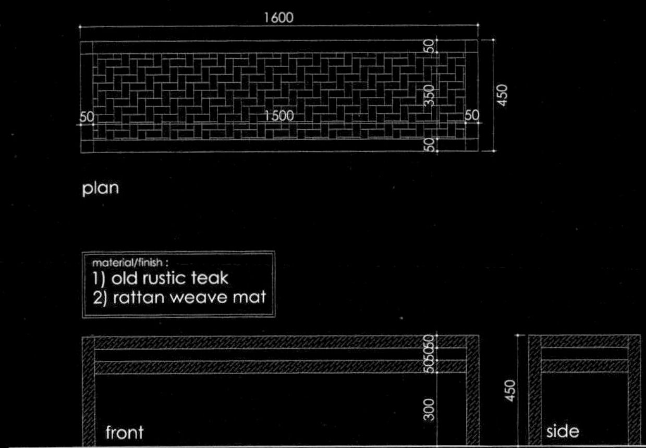

Bench.

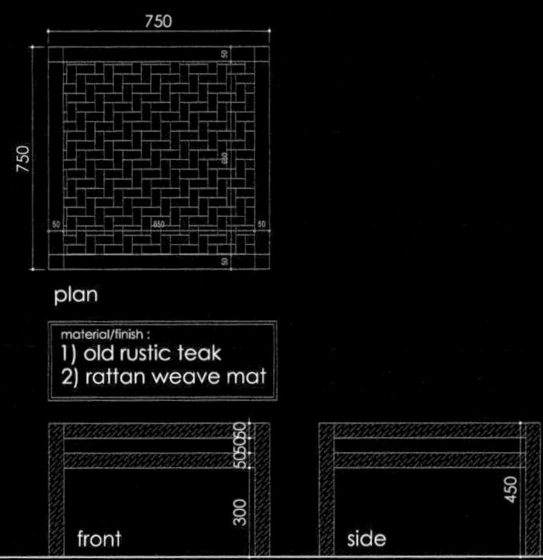

Small Table.

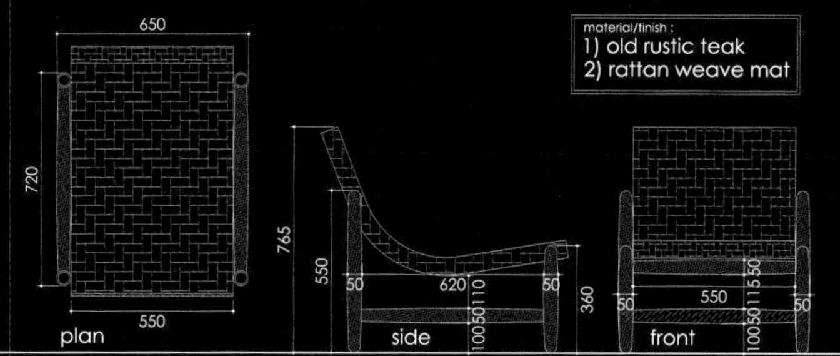

Sleigh Chair.

View of bathroom at private Villa with open garden. Bathtub & vanity counter were custom made.

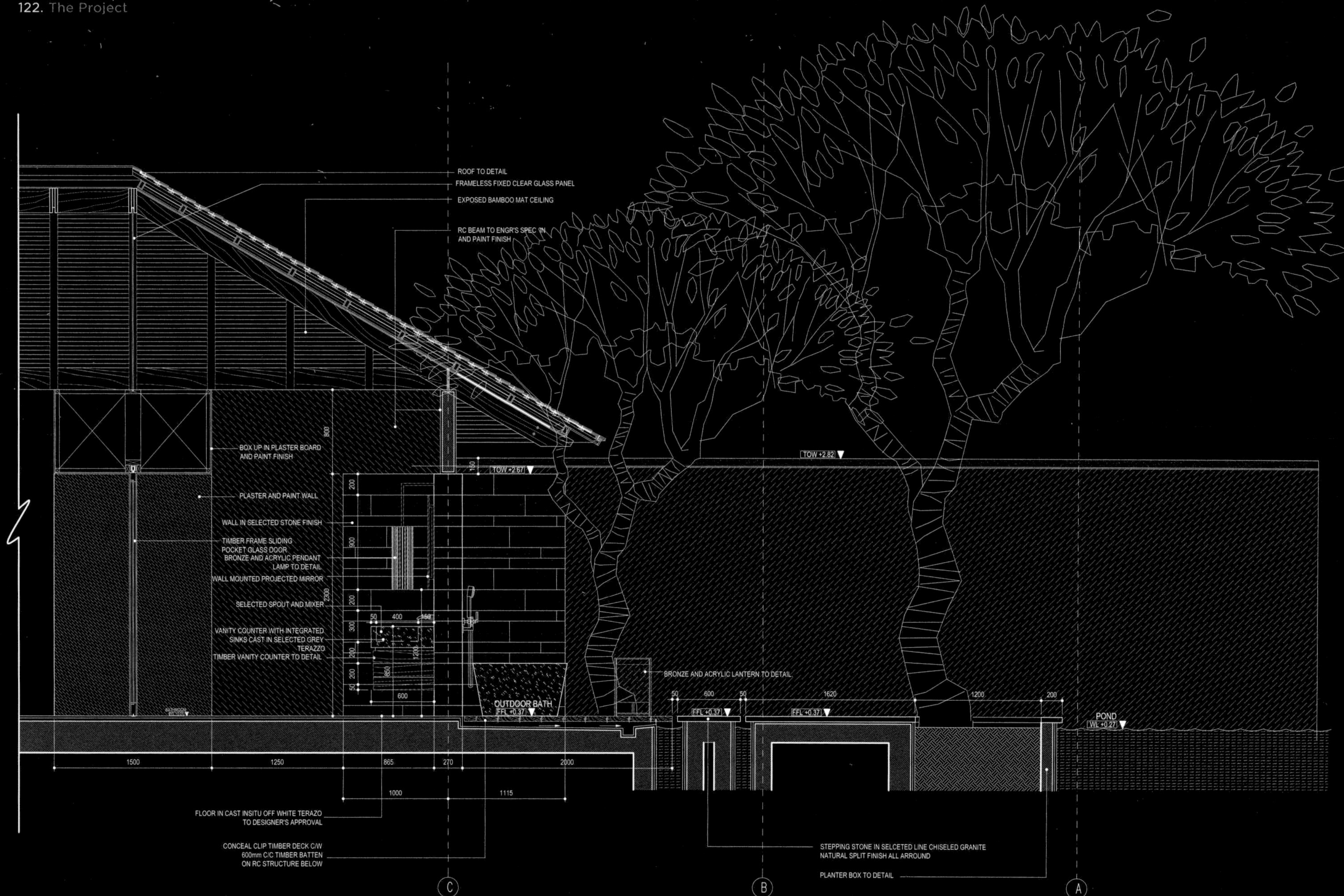

Sections of Guest Bathroom 4.

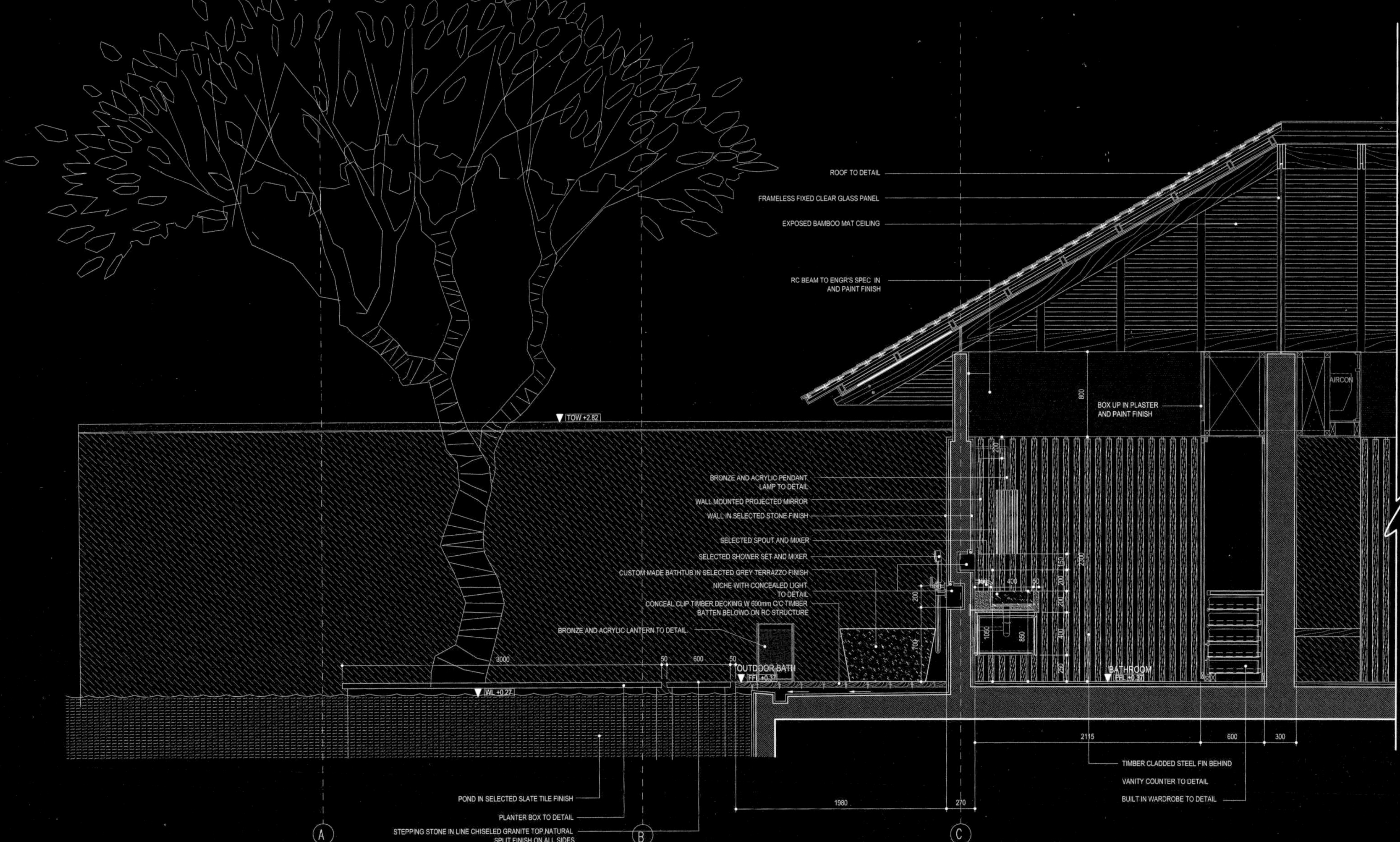
ROOF TO DETAIL
FRAMELESS FIXED CLEAR GLASS PANEL
EXPOSED BAMBOO MAT CEILING
RC BEAM TO ENGR'S SPEC IN AND PAINT FINISH
BOX UP IN PLASTER AND PAINT FINISH
AIRCON
800
TOW +2.82
BRONZE AND ACRYLIC PENDANT LAMP TO DETAIL
WALL MOUNTED PROJECTED MIRROR
WALL IN SELECTED STONE FINISH
SELECTED SPOUT AND MIXER
SELECTED SHOWER SET AND MIXER
CUSTOM MADE BATHTUB IN SELECTED GREY TERRAZZO FINISH
NICHE WITH CONCEALED LIGHT TO DETAIL
CONCEAL CLIP TIMBER DECKING W 600mm C/C TIMBER BATTEN BELOWO ON RC STRUCTURE
BRONZE AND ACRYLIC LANTERN TO DETAIL
3000
50
600
50
OUTDOOR BATH
FFL +0.37
WL +0.27
BATHROOM
FFL +0.37
2300
1050
850
700
2115
600
300
TIMBER CLADDED STEEL FIN BEHIND
VANITY COUNTER TO DETAIL
BUILT IN WARDROBE TO DETAIL
1980
270
POND IN SELECTED SLATE TILE FINISH
PLANTER BOX TO DETAIL
STEPPING STONE IN LINE CHISELED GRANITE TOP,NATURAL SPLIT FINISH ON ALL SIDES
A
B
C

Early view of private fish pond outside bathroom area

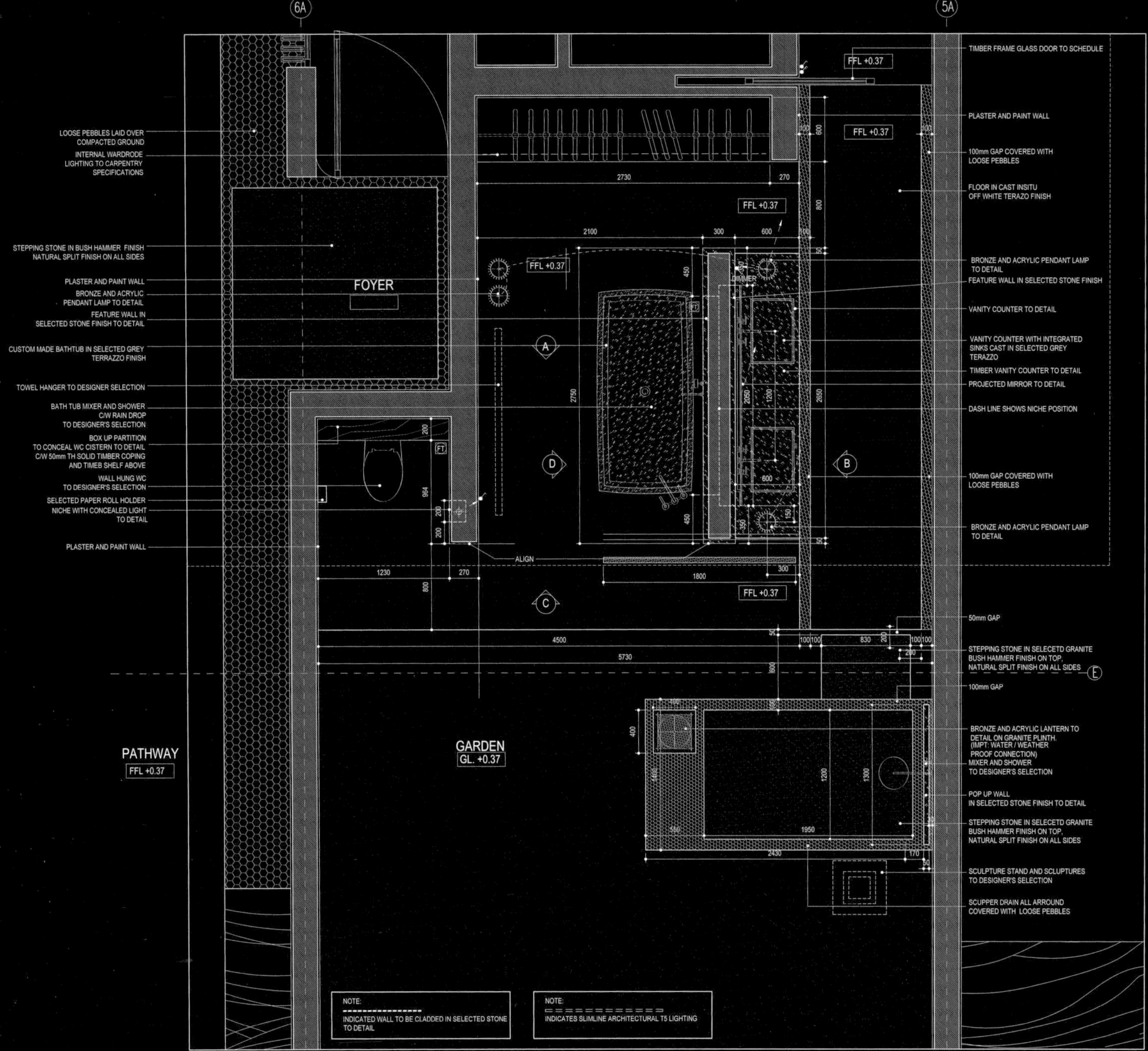

Plan of Guest Bathroom 1

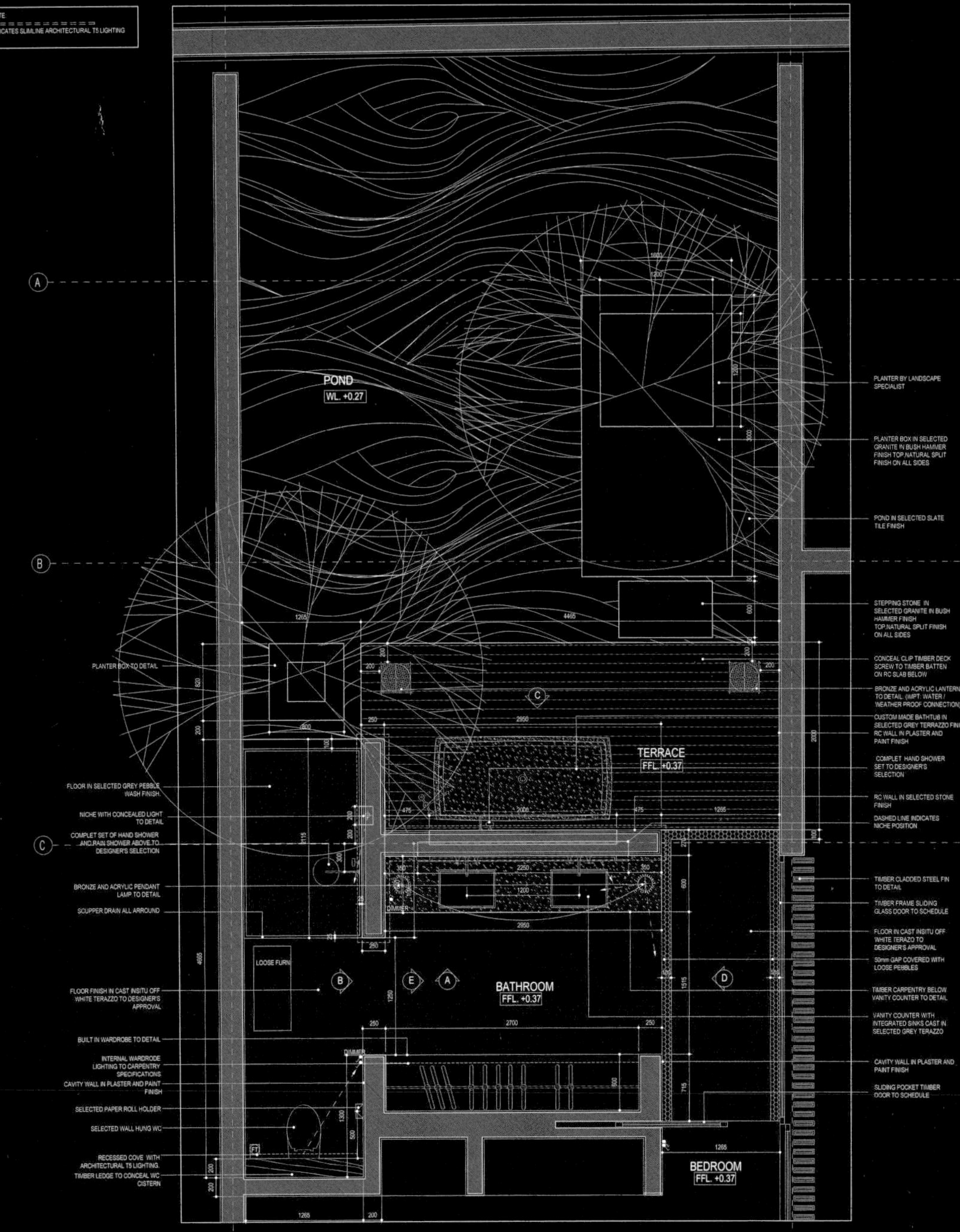
ICATES SLIMLINE ARCHITECTURAL T5 LIGHTING
POND
WL. +0.27
TERRACE
FFL. +0.37
BATHROOM
FFL. +0.37
BEDROOM
FFL. +0.37
LOOSE FURN
DIMMER
PLANTER BY LANDSCAPE SPECIALIST
PLANTER BOX IN SELECTED GRANITE IN BUSH HAMMER FINISH TOP,NATURAL SPLIT FINISH ON ALL SIDES
POND IN SELECTED SLATE TILE FINISH
STEPPING STONE IN SELECTED GRANITE IN BUSH HAMMER FINISH TOP,NATURAL SPLIT FINISH ON ALL SIDES
CONCEAL CLIP TIMBER DECK SCREW TO TIMBER BATTEN ON RC SLAB BELOW
BRONZE AND ACRYLIC LANTERN TO DETAIL (IMPT: WATER / WEATHER PROOF CONNECTION)
CUSTOM MADE BATHTUB IN SELECTED GREY TERRAZZO FINI
RC WALL IN PLASTER AND PAINT FINISH
COMPLET HAND SHOWER SET TO DESIGNER'S SELECTION
RC WALL IN SELECTED STONE FINISH
DASHED LINE INDICATES NICHE POSITION
TIMBER CLADDED STEEL FIN TO DETAIL
TIMBER FRAME SLIDING GLASS DOOR TO SCHEDULE
FLOOR IN CAST INSITU OFF WHITE TERAZO TO DESIGNER'S APPROVAL
50mm GAP COVERED WITH LOOSE PEBBLES
TIMBER CARPENTRY BELOW VANITY COUNTER TO DETAIL
VANITY COUNTER WITH INTEGRATED SINKS CAST IN SELECTED GREY TERRAZZO
CAVITY WALL IN PLASTER AND PAINT FINISH
SLIDING POCKET TIMBER DOOR TO SCHEDULE
PLANTER BOX TO DETAIL
FLOOR IN SELECTED GREY PEBBLE WASH FINISH.
NICHE WITH CONCEALED LIGHT TO DETAIL
COMPLET SET OF HAND SHOWER AND RAIN SHOWER ABOVE TO DESIGNER'S SELECTION
BRONZE AND ACRYLIC PENDANT LAMP TO DETAIL
SCUPPER DRAIN ALL ARROUND
FLOOR FINISH IN CAST INSITU OFF WHITE TERAZZO TO DESIGNER'S APPROVAL
BUILT IN WARDROBE TO DETAIL
INTERNAL WARDRODE LIGHTING TO CARPENTRY SPECIFICATIONS
CAVITY WALL IN PLASTER AND PAINT FINISH
SELECTED PAPER ROLL HOLDER
SELECTED WALL HUNG WC
RECESSED COVE WITH ARCHITECTURAL T5 LIGHTING.
TIMBER LEDGE TO CONCEAL WC CISTERN

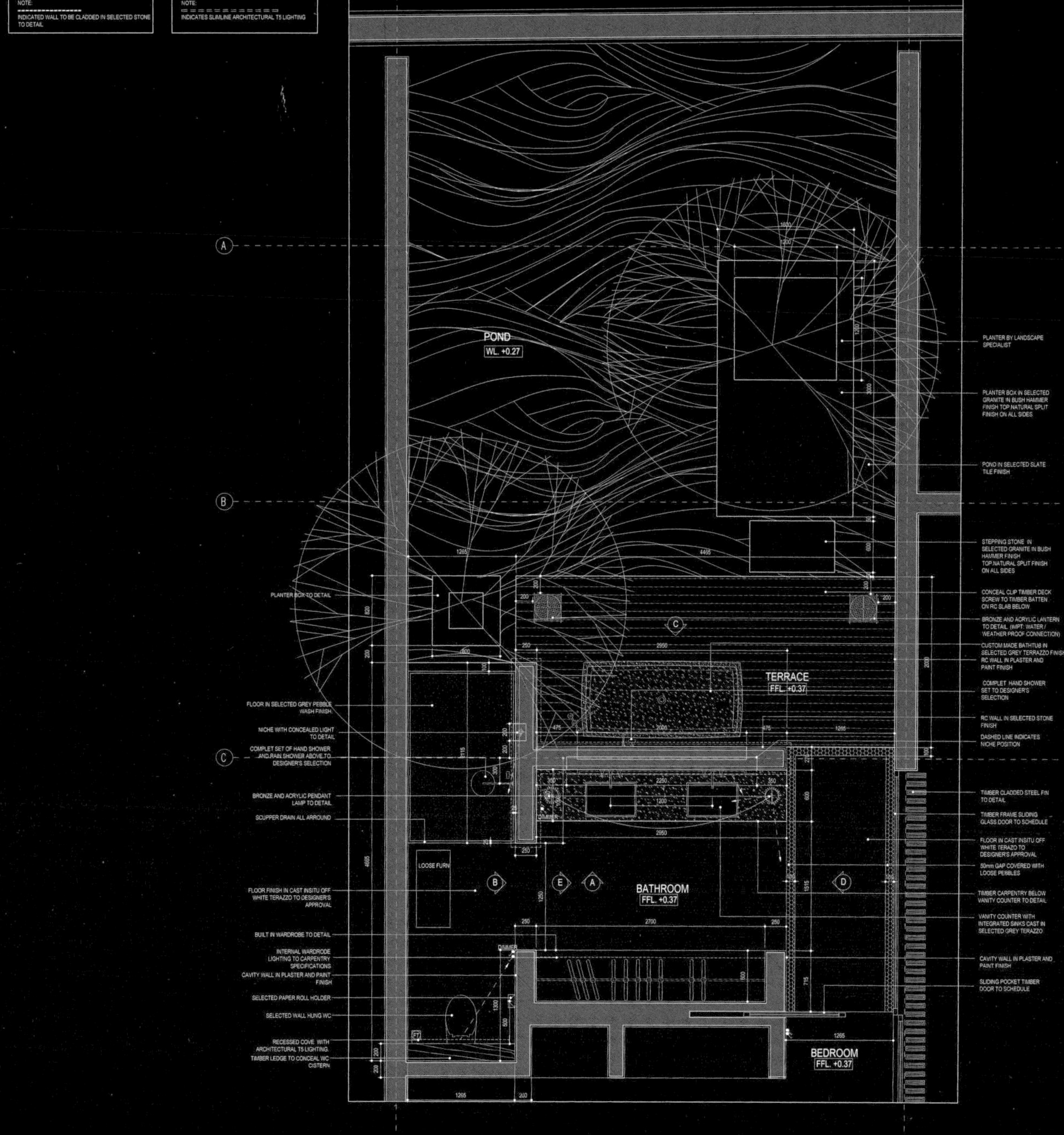

Plan of Guest Bathroom 4.

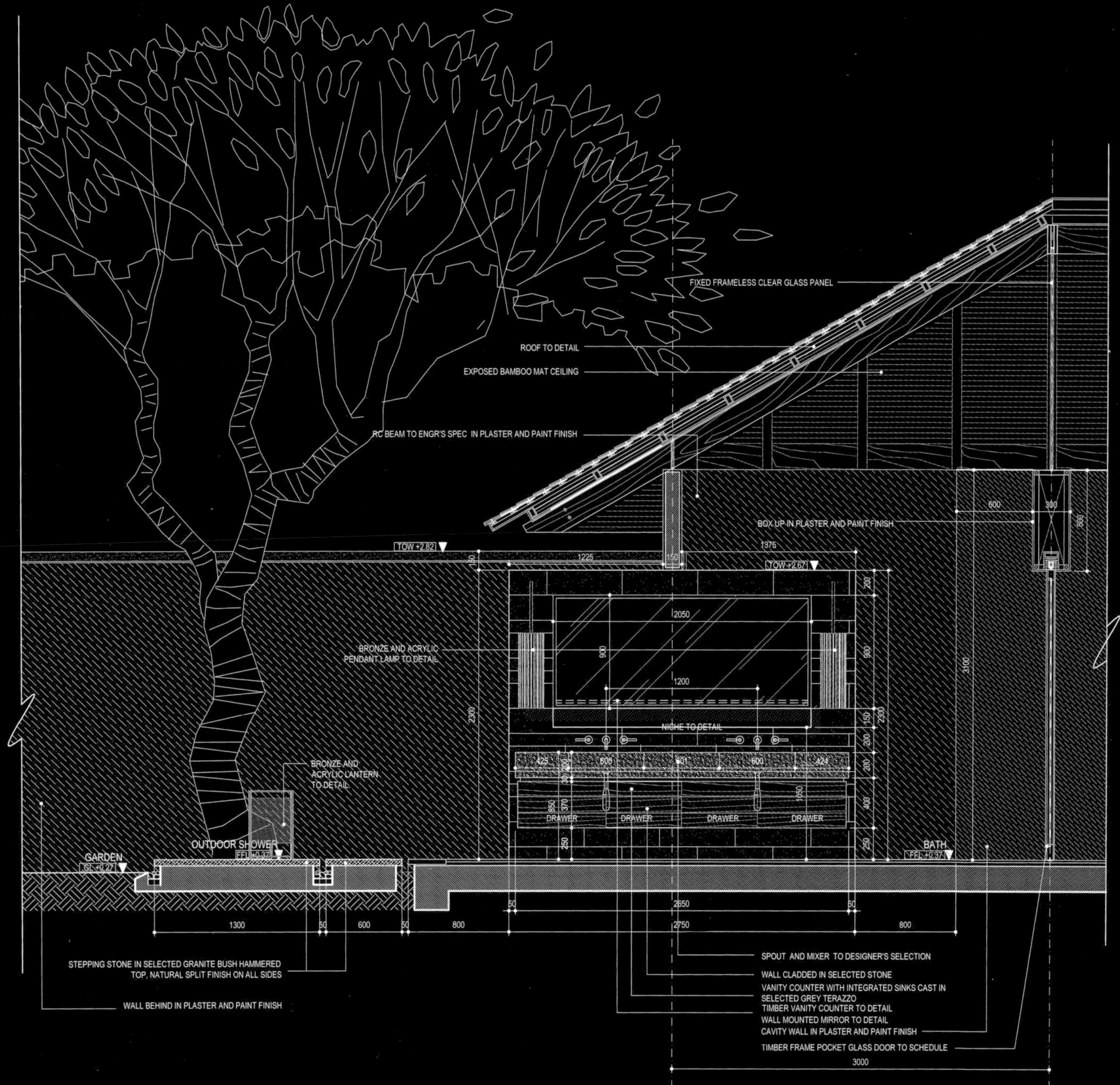
FIXED FRAMELESS CLEAR GLASS PANEL
ROOF TO DETAIL
EXPOSED BAMBOO MAT CEILING
RC BEAM TO ENGR'S SPEC IN PLASTER AND PAINT FINISH
BOX UP IN PLASTER AND PAINT FINISH
TOW +2.82
TOW +2.67
BRONZE AND ACRYLIC PENDANT LAMP TO DETAIL
NICHE TO DETAIL
DRAWER
DRAWER
DRAWER
DRAWER
BRONZE AND ACRYLIC LANTERN TO DETAIL
GARDEN
OUTDOOR SHOWER
BATH
STEPPING STONE IN SELECTED GRANITE BUSH HAMMERED TOP, NATURAL SPLIT FINISH ON ALL SIDES
WALL BEHIND IN PLASTER AND PAINT FINISH
SPOUT AND MIXER TO DESIGNER'S SELECTION
WALL CLADDED IN SELECTED STONE
VANITY COUNTER WITH INTEGRATED SINKS CAST IN SELECTED GREY TERAZZO
TIMBER VANITY COUNTER TO DETAIL
WALL MOUNTED MIRROR TO DETAIL
CAVITY WALL IN PLASTER AND PAINT FINISH
TIMBER FRAME POCKET GLASS DOOR TO SCHEDULE
1300
600
800
2750
800
3000

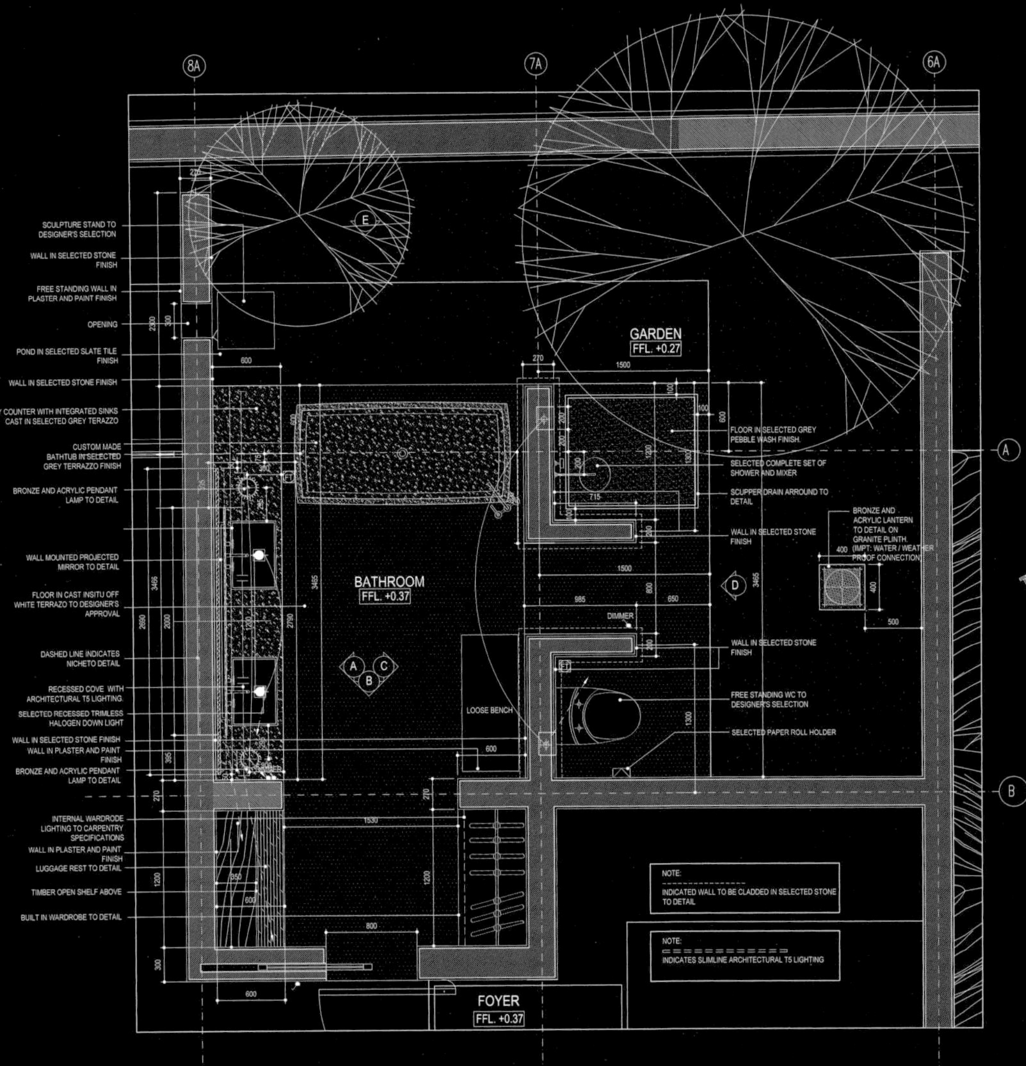
8A
7A
6A
SCULPTURE STAND TO DESIGNER'S SELECTION
WALL IN SELECTED STONE FINISH
FREE STANDING WALL IN PLASTER AND PAINT FINISH
OPENING
POND IN SELECTED SLATE TILE FINISH
WALL IN SELECTED STONE FINISH
COUNTER WITH INTEGRATED SINKS CAST IN SELECTED GREY TERRAZZO
CUSTOM MADE BATHTUB IN SELECTED GREY TERRAZZO FINISH
BRONZE AND ACRYLIC PENDANT LAMP TO DETAIL
WALL MOUNTED PROJECTED MIRROR TO DETAIL
FLOOR IN CAST INSITU OFF WHITE TERAZZO TO DESIGNER'S APPROVAL
DASHED LINE INDICATES NICHETO DETAIL
RECESSED COVE WITH ARCHITECTURAL T5 LIGHTING
SELECTED RECESSED TRIMLESS HALOGEN DOWN LIGHT
WALL IN SELECTED STONE FINISH
WALL IN PLASTER AND PAINT FINISH
BRONZE AND ACRYLIC PENDANT LAMP TO DETAIL
INTERNAL WARDRODE LIGHTING TO CARPENTRY SPECIFICATIONS
WALL IN PLASTER AND PAINT FINISH
LUGGAGE REST TO DETAIL
TIMBER OPEN SHELF ABOVE
BUILT IN WARDROBE TO DETAIL
GARDEN
FFL. +0.27
BATHROOM
FFL. +0.37
FOYER
FFL. +0.37
LOOSE BENCH
DIMMER
FLOOR IN SELECTED GREY PEBBLE WASH FINISH
SELECTED COMPLETE SET OF SHOWER AND MIXER
SCUPPER DRAIN ARROUND TO DETAIL
WALL IN SELECTED STONE FINISH
BRONZE AND ACRYLIC LANTERN TO DETAIL ON GRANITE PLINTH (IMPT: WATER / WEATHER PROOF CONNECTION)
WALL IN SELECTED STONE FINISH
FREE STANDING WC TO DESIGNER'S SELECTION
SELECTED PAPER ROLL HOLDER
NOTE:
INDICATED WALL TO BE CLADDED IN SELECTED STONE TO DETAIL
NOTE:
INDICATES SLIMLINE ARCHITECTURAL T5 LIGHTING

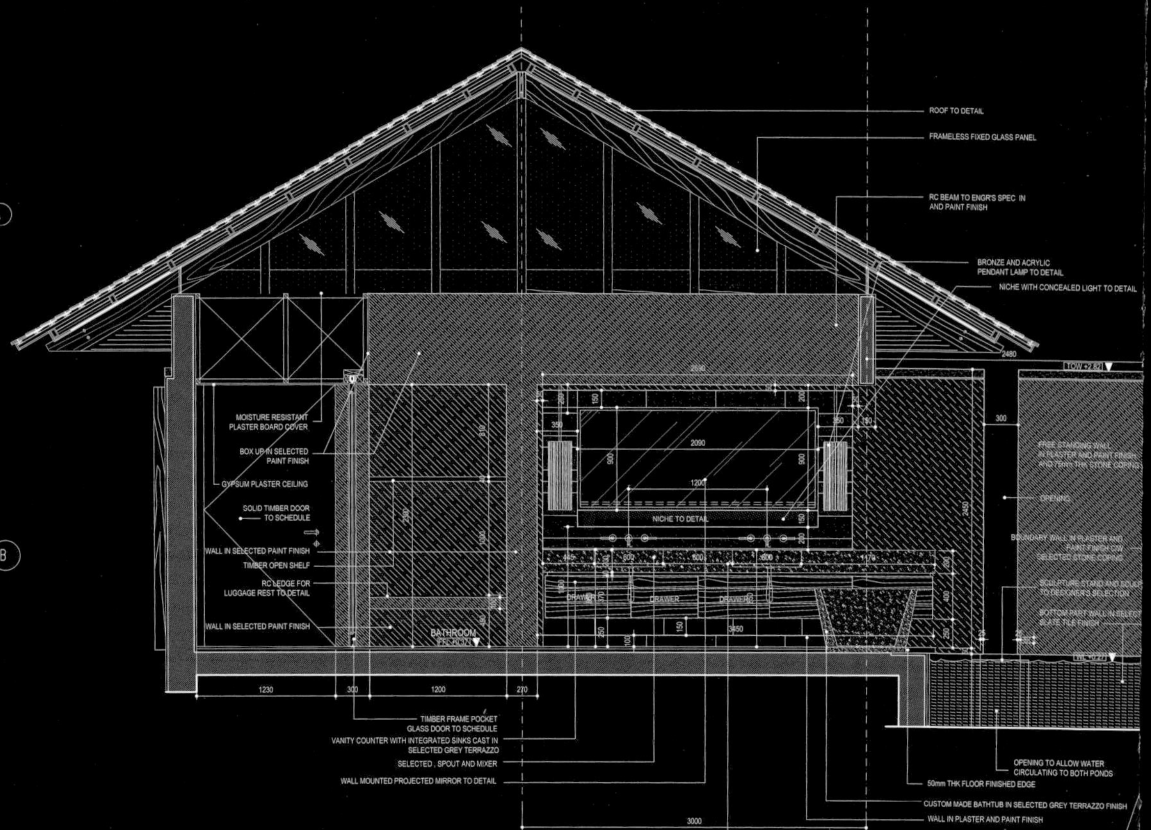
ROOF TO DETAIL
FRAMELESS FIXED GLASS PANEL
RC BEAM TO ENGR'S SPEC IN AND PAINT FINISH
BRONZE AND ACRYLIC PENDANT LAMP TO DETAIL
NICHE WITH CONCEALED LIGHT TO DETAIL
MOISTURE RESISTANT PLASTER BOARD COVER
BOX UP IN SELECTED PAINT FINISH
GYPSUM PLASTER CEILING
SOLID TIMBER DOOR TO SCHEDULE
WALL IN SELECTED PAINT FINISH
TIMBER OPEN SHELF
RC LEDGE FOR LUGGAGE REST TO DETAIL
WALL IN SELECTED PAINT FINISH
NICHE TO DETAIL
DRAWER
BATHROOM
TIMBER FRAME POCKET GLASS DOOR TO SCHEDULE
VANITY COUNTER WITH INTEGRATED SINKS CAST IN SELECTED GREY TERRAZZO
SELECTED , SPOUT AND MIXER
WALL MOUNTED PROJECTED MIRROR TO DETAIL
OPENING TO ALLOW WATER CIRCULATING TO BOTH PONDS
50mm THK FLOOR FINISHED EDGE
CUSTOM MADE BATHTUB IN SELECTED GREY TERRAZZO FINISH
WALL IN PLASTER AND PAINT FINISH

View of bathroom in a private Villa with open garden. Bathtub & vanity counter were custom made.

Sections of Guest Bathroom 1.

View of Main Villa at night.

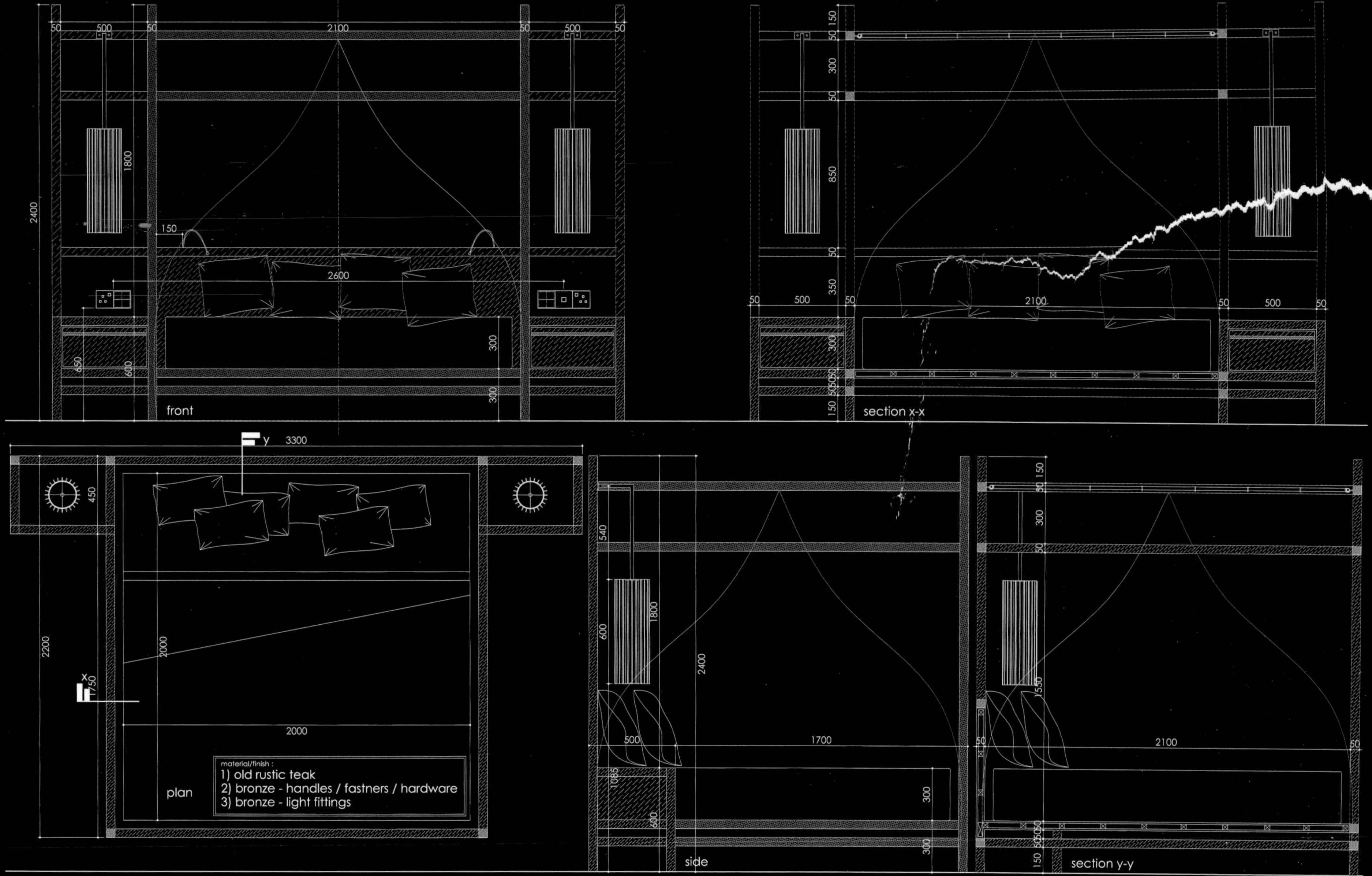

The bed in the Master Pavilion.

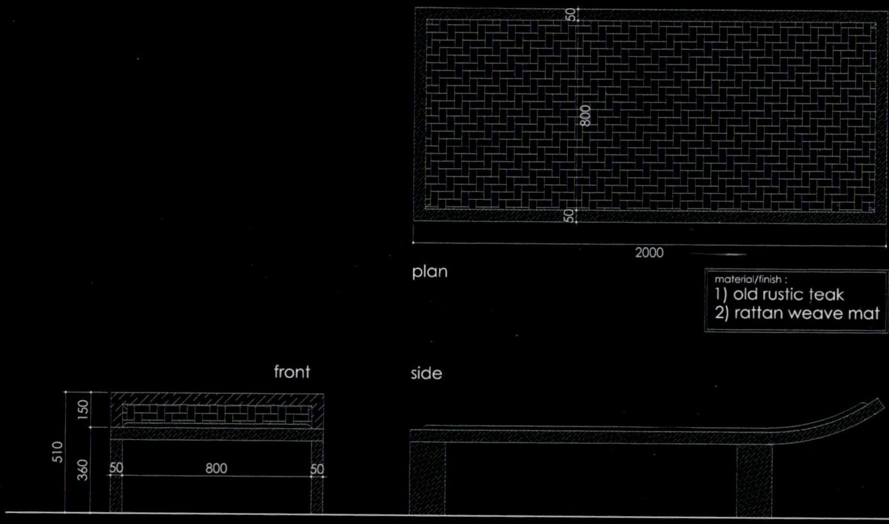

Lounger.

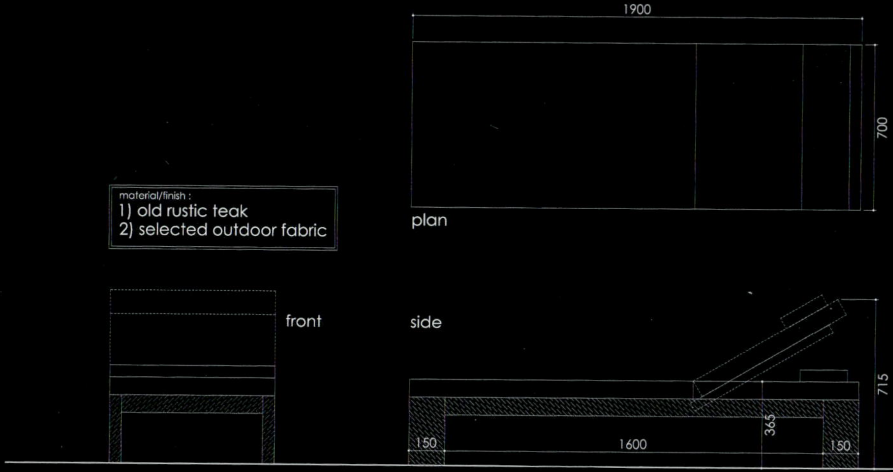

Sun Lounger (single)

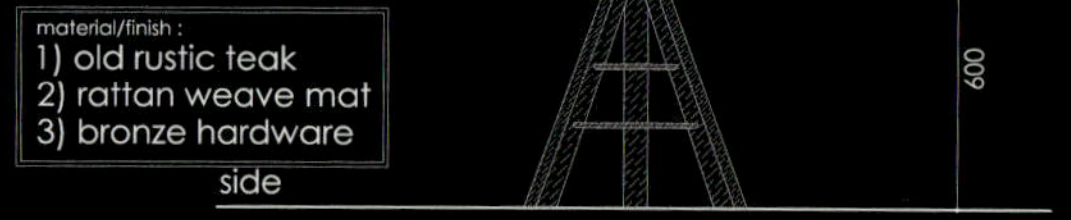

Low Square Table.

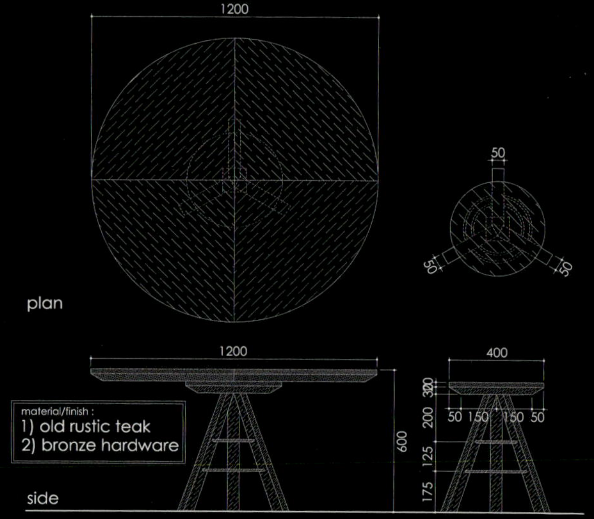

Low Round Table.

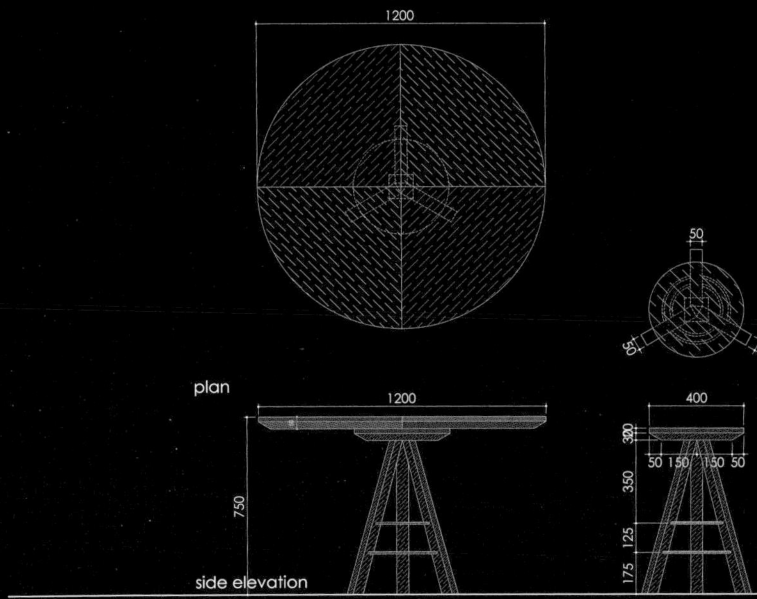

Round Table.

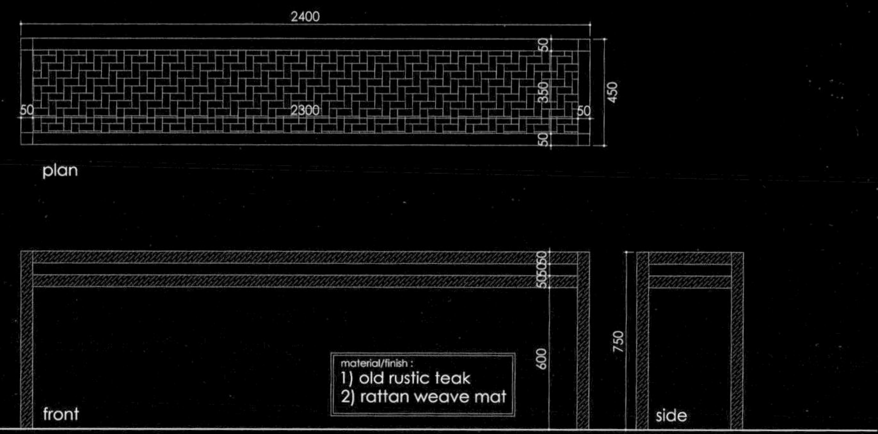

Console.

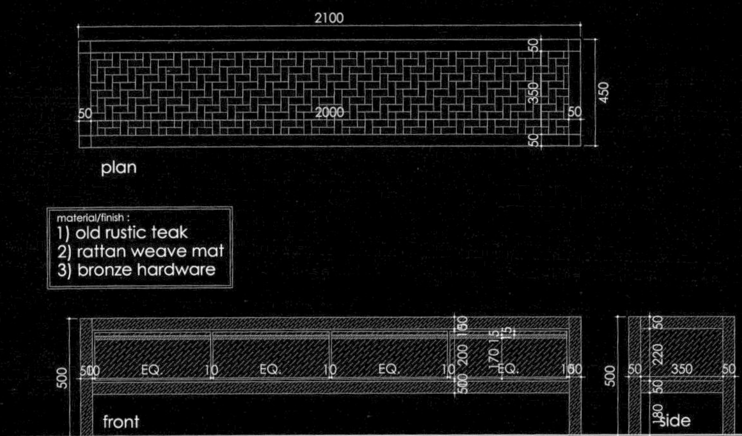

TV Console.

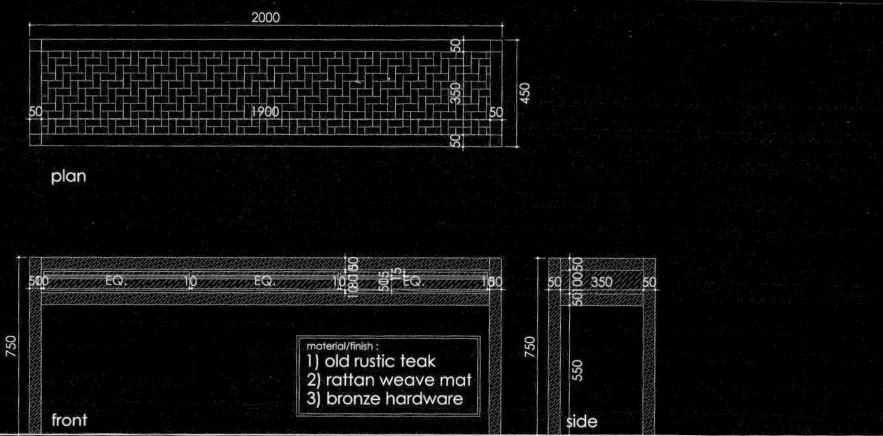

Vanity Table.

Overall view of the Villa at dusk.

Sections of the Master Bedroom.

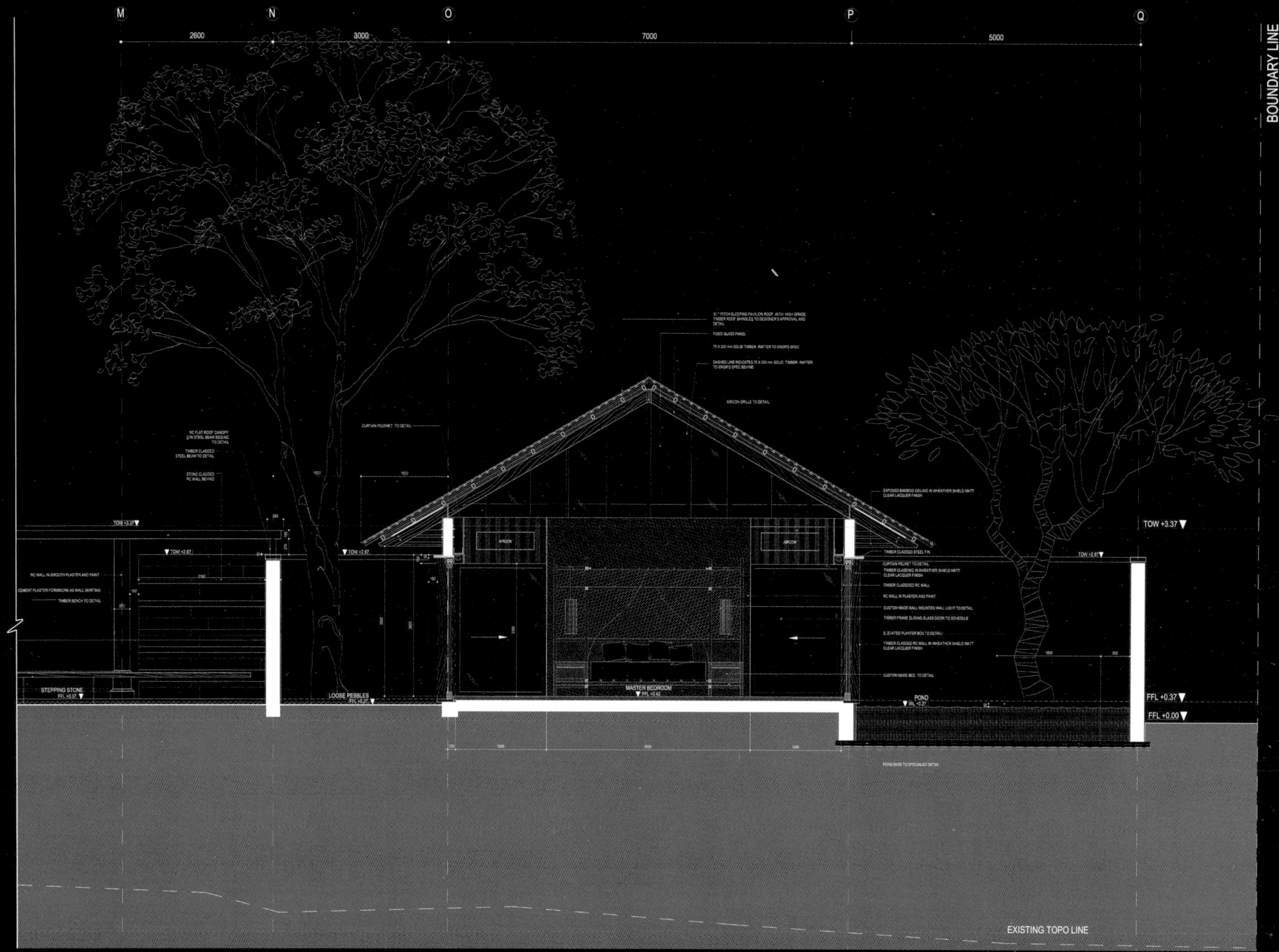

Sections of the Master Bedroom.

View of Main Guest Living/Dining Pavilions at dusk from the swimming pool.

Evening views of Main Living Pavilion.

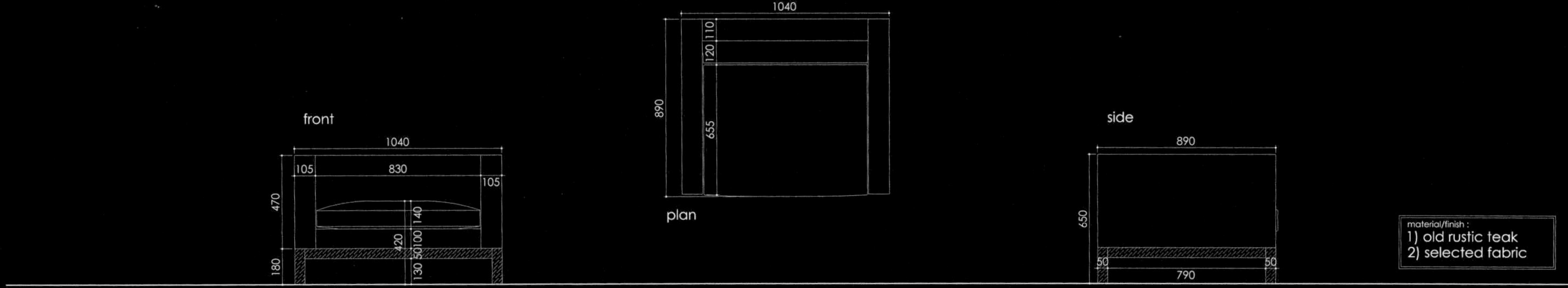

material/finish :
1) old rustic teak
2) selected fabric

Fabric Armchair.

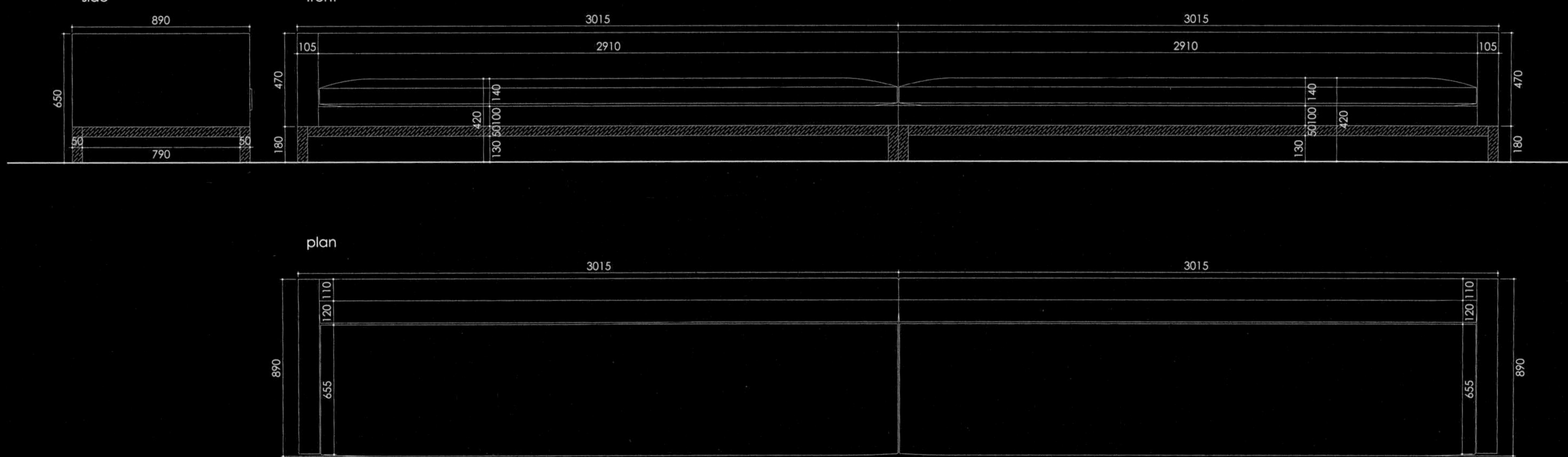

Mixed Sofa.

material/finish :
1) old rustic teak
2) selected fabric

Evening views of Main Living Pavilion.

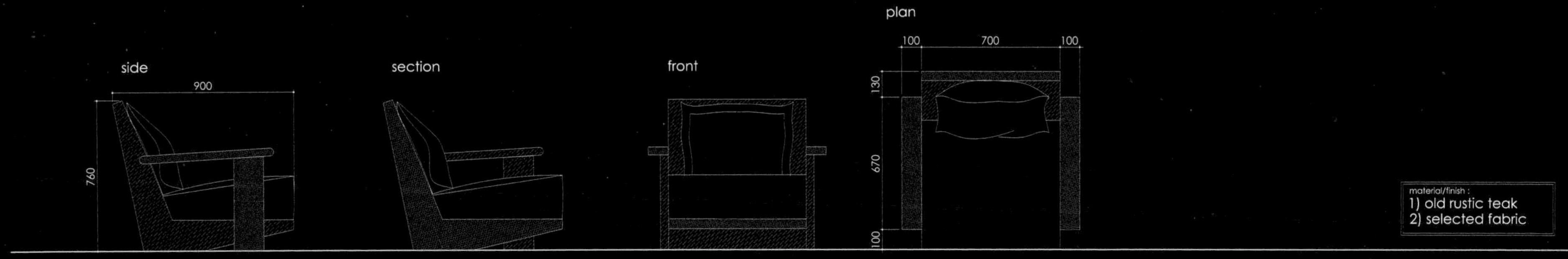

Mixed Armchair.

Mixed Sofa.

Evening views of Main Living Pavilion.

Entry view of Main Pavilion in the evening.

Night views of entry circulation.

Night view of Entry Court & detail views of circulations.

Night view of Entry Court & detail views of circulations.

/02
Drawings

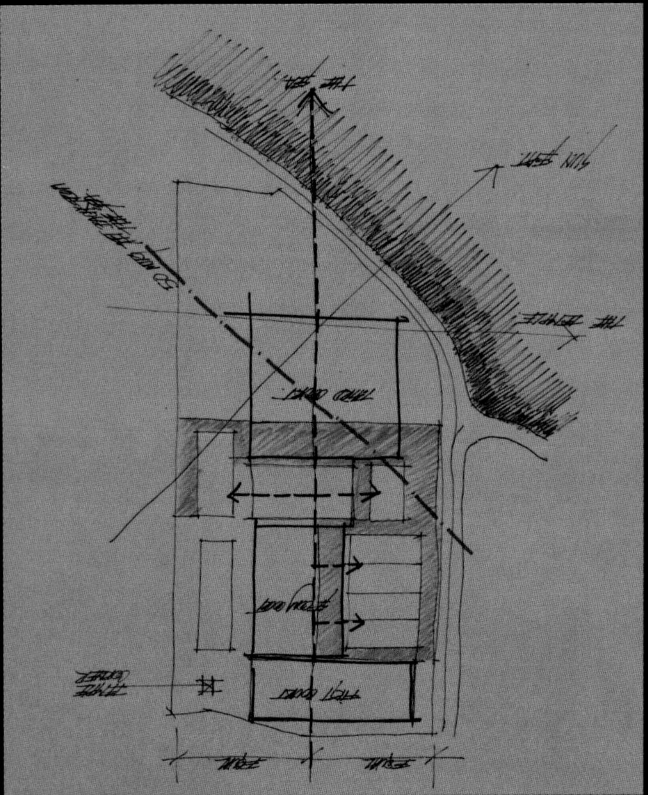
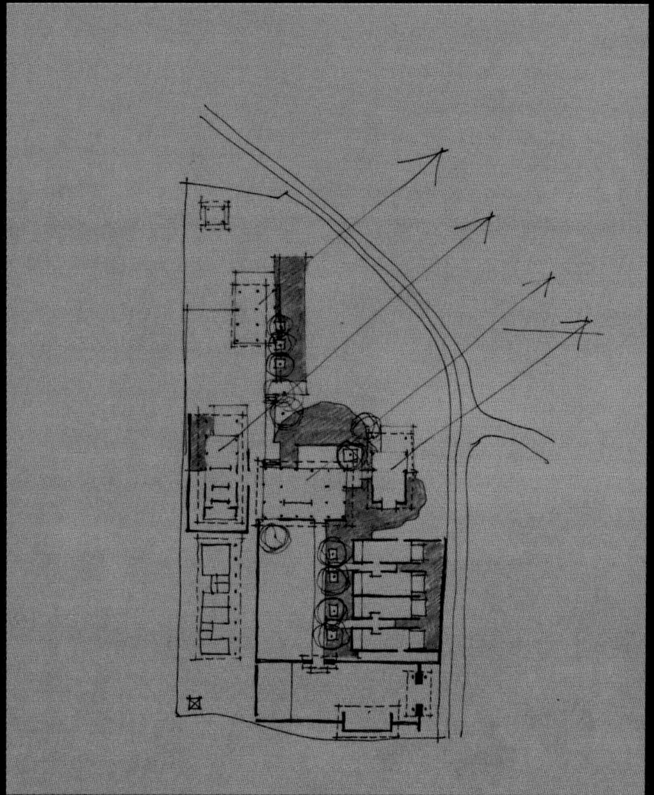
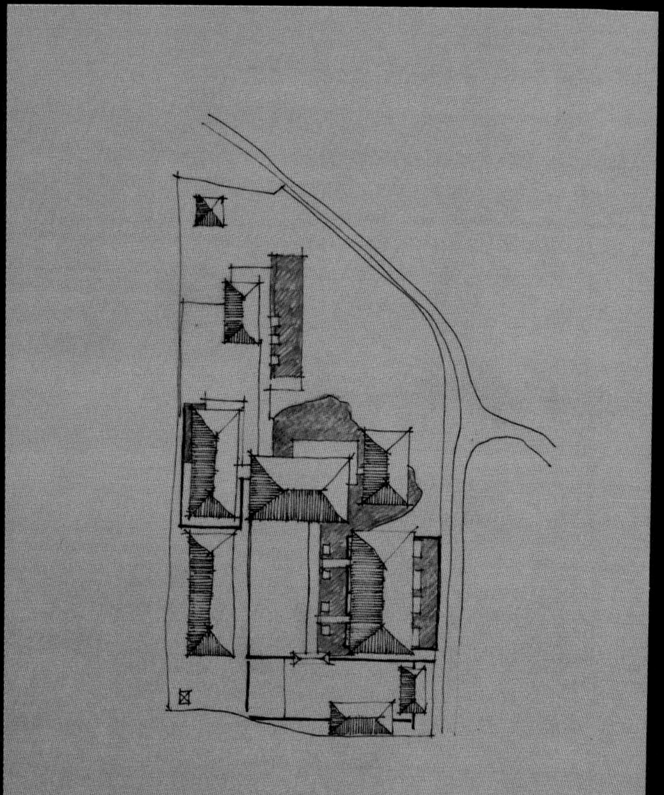

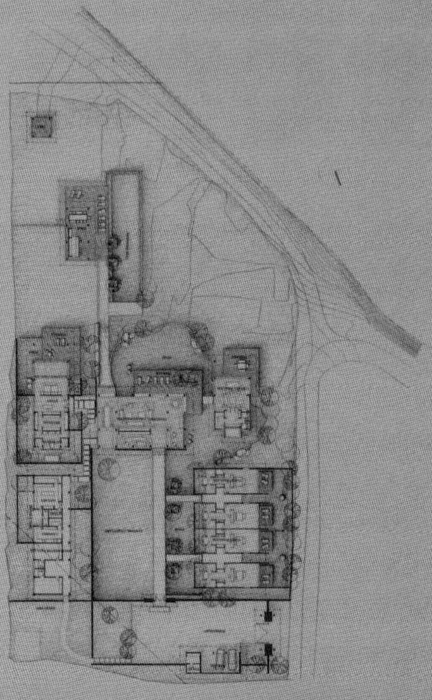
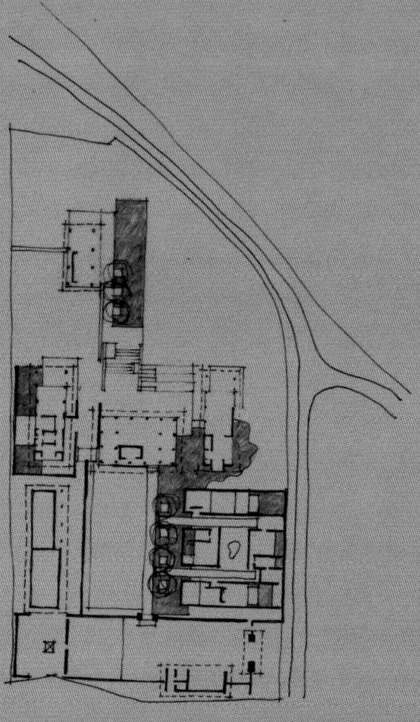
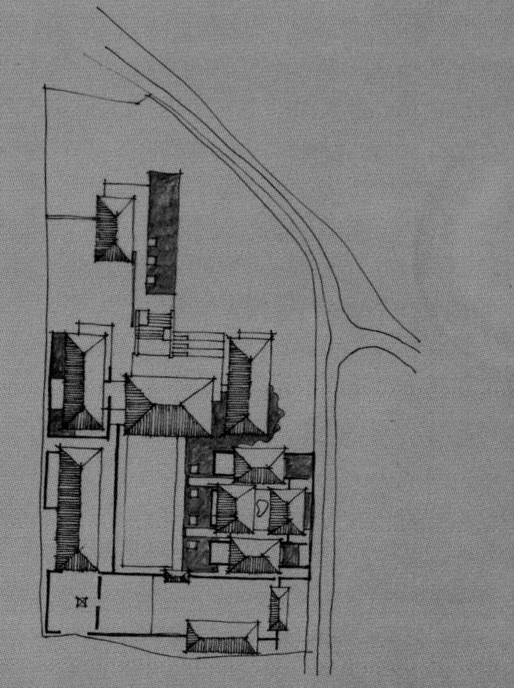

First Floor Plan

1 driveway
2 forecourt
3 garage
4 guard house
5 spirit house
6 back yard
7 generator room
8 electrical room
9 pump room
10 maids room
11 house keeper living
12 laundry
13 service yard
14 kitchen
15 store
16 pond
17 master bath
18 dressing
19 study
20 sleeping pavilion
21 terrace
22 pantry
23 principal living pavilion
24 swimming pool
25 bale
26 garden
27 library pavilion
28 gym
29 lotus pond
30 guest pavilion
31 central court yard
32 sea

32
1
16
16
16
30
30
21
27
28
30
2
30
3
16
4
29
29
29
23
21
24
22
31
25
21
20
19
18
17
14
12
11
10
7
5
15
10
10
8
9
16
13
6

Roof Plan.

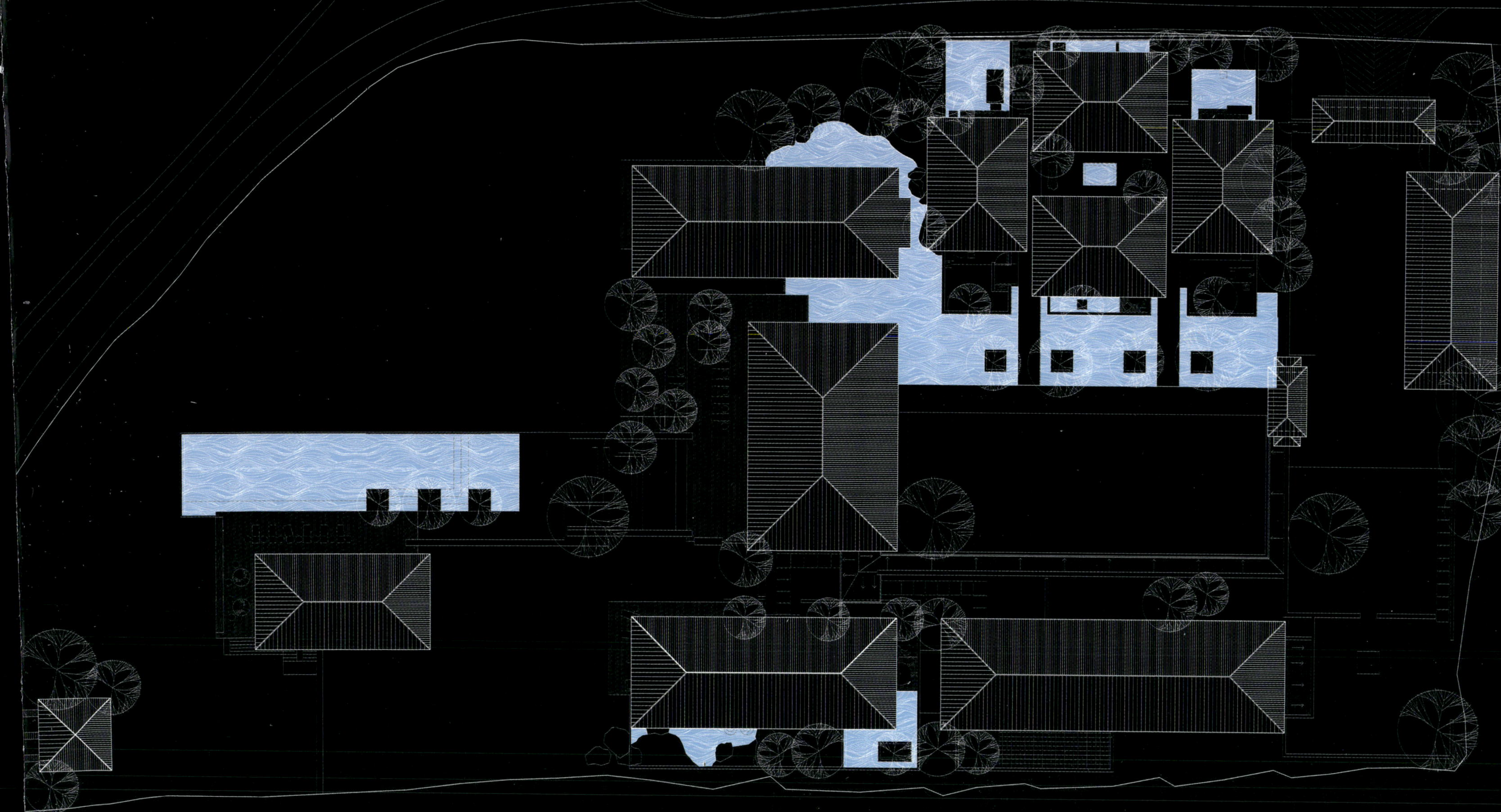

Elevations.

SPLAYED BOUNDARY LINE
BOUNDARY LINE BEHIND

BOUNDARY LINE BEHIND
BOUNDARY LINE
BOUNDARY LINE

Elevations.

SPLAYED BOUNDARY LINE
BOUNDARY LINE BEHIND

SPLAYED BOUNDARY LINE

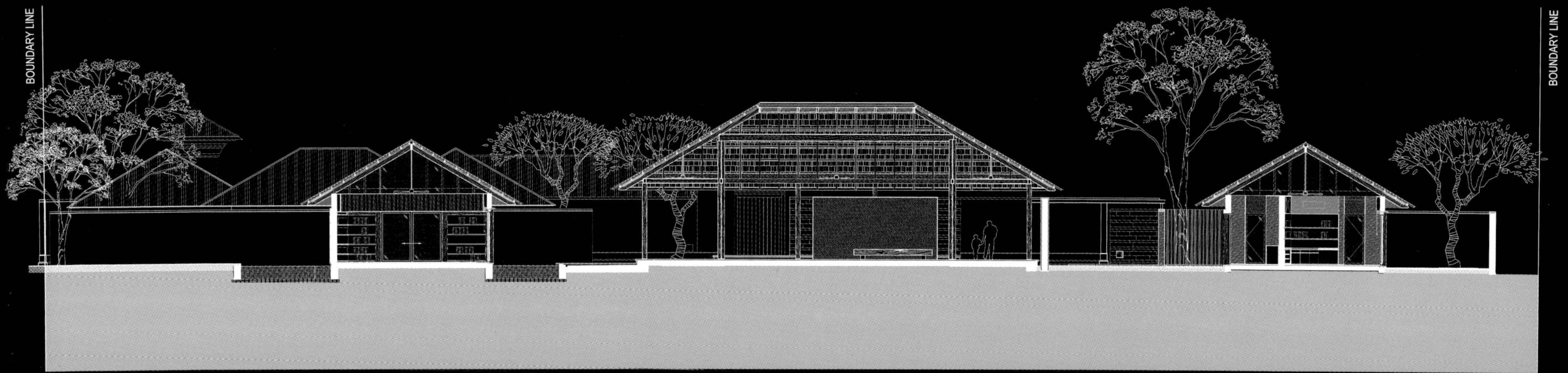
BOUNDARY LINE
BOUNDARY LINE

/03

Site and Construction

MEP TEAM

/04

Project Data

Name:	The Jiva Puri
Location:	Jalan Pantai Mengening Desa Cemagi, Kecamatan Badung Bali, Indonesia
Year of Design:	2008
Year of Construction:	2009-2010
Size of the Lot:	8,233 sqm, 88,511 sqf
Size of the Building:	1,389 sqm, 14,932 sqf
Project Team:	Mr. Ernesto Bedmar, Bedmar & Shi, Design Consultant Ms. Shinta Siregar, Nexus Studio Architect, Local Architect Mr. Made Sudiadnya, Project Manager
Interior Designer:	Mr. Ernesto Bedmar, Bedmar & Shi, Mr. Gavin Pennefather, Interior Designer
Landscape Architect:	Mr. Trevor Hiller, One Degree North
Consultants:	Mr. Arief Soetrisno, Structural Engineer, PT Atelier Enam Struktur Mr. Lukito Pramono, M&E Engineer, CV. Lintas Daya Mr. Kadek Mahaenu, Quantity Surveyor, PT Cipta Pesona Sentosa Sejahtera/CPSS
Contractor:	Mr. Paul Tendean, PT Cipta Kreasi Bangun Pratama (CKBP)

Ernesto Bedmar, an Argentinian, graduated with a Bachelor of Architecture degree in 1980 from the University of Architecture & Town Planning, Cordoba, Argentina; he received the award for the Best Design in the Final Year. He is a Registered Architect in Argentina and also a Registered Architect in Singapore, as well as a Corporate Member of the Singapore Institute of Architects. Ernesto's career began in 1977 when he did practical work in the studio of Miguel Angel Roca, Argentina. In 1980 he became an Associate at Miguel Angel Roca, South Africa, and designed a town planning project for Protea New Town – South Africa and the Jabulani Administrative Centre in South Africa where he worked with the Architects M.A. Roca and F. Pienaar. In 1982 he was made an Associate at Miguel Angel Roca, Hong Kong, to develop the Tai Long Wan Tourist Resort on Lantau Island, HK. He then joined Palmer & Turner, Hong Kong as a Consultant Architect in 1983 and was involved in a vast urban project for Macau as a member of the planning group under the Architect Alvaro Siza Vieira.

In 1984 he came to Singapore and worked with SAA Partnership until 1986 when he set up his own practice; Bedmar & Shi Designers Pte Ltd, and since then has been a Director/Design Consultant at the company. From 1989 to 2000 Ernesto was a part-time tutor at the School of Architecture at the National University of Singapore and from 1993 to 1995 he was a Member of Design Committee at Temasek Polytechnic, Singapore, where he also acted as External Examiner for the Bachelor of Arts (Architecture/Hons) program from 2007 to 2010.

In early 2009 Ernesto was invited by the Architecture Society at The National University of Singapore to give a guest lecture and in May 2009 he was invited by Raffles University, Singapore, to act as an External Examiner for Design Programmes.

He has received several awards including some listed here in chronological order:

1989. Du Pont Antron Design Award – Honorary Prize – Store Planning Category.
2000. No. 15 Whitehouse Park – Architectural Heritage Awards (URA).
2002. Merit Prize (from the Singapore Institute of Architects – Hunter Douglas Design Competition).
2006. 3 Houses at Jervois and Trevose 12 – The Chicago Athenaeum International Architecture Award.
2006. Cityscape Architectural Review Awards.
2006. Dubai – Winner of Residential Built Award.
2010. 10 th SIA Architectural Design Awards in the categories for Recreational Buildings and Individual Houses.
2011. The Asia Pacific Property Awards for The Jiva Puri interiors.

Besides his monograph "Romancing the Tropics" also published by Oscar Riera Ojeda, Ernesto's works have been featured in many international publications.

Firm profile

Bedmar & Shi is a Singapore based design practice established in 1986, incorporating a wide range of architectural, conservation, landscape and interior designs.

Since its inception, it has always maintained a staff of twelve; a multicultural mix of personalities from various parts of the world, designers with a singular desire to explore the relationships between buildings and nature with a particular emphasis on quality design and execution of its diverse portfolio.

The company founders, Mr. Ernesto Bedmar and Madam Patti Shi, personally liaise and direct each of the company's projects.

Their portfolio includes works in New York, London, New Zealand, India, Malaysia, Indonesia, Thailand, Tibet, Bhutan, Hong Kong and Singapore.

Book Credits

Creative Direction by Leo Malinow
Graphic Design by Ale Román
Copy Editing by Kit Maude

ISBN 978-988-16195-1-8
Printed in China.

OSCAR RIERA OJEDA PUBLISHERS LIMITED
Unit 1A 20/F.,
Far East Consortium Bldg.,
121 Des Voeux Rd Central, Hong Kong.
T: +852-5311-1625

EDITORIAL OFFICES | USA
143 South 2ND Street, Suite 208
Philadelphia PA 19106-3073

PRODUCTION OFFICES | CHINA
Park A, Fang Da Cheng, Longjing Belhuan Avenue,
Nanshan District, Shenzhen 518055
T:+86-182-0098-3774

www.oropublishers.com | www.oscarrieraojeda.com
oscar@oscarrieraojeda.com